Name It! Claim It!
Take It!

DAG HEWARD-MILLS

Parchment House

Copyright © 2008 Dag Heward-Mills

First published 2008
by Lux Verbi B.M. (Pty) Ltd

ISBN 13: 978-0-7963-0810-8

3rd Printing 2014 by Parchment House

Find out more about Dag Heward-Mills at:

Healing Jesus Campaign
Write to: evangelist@daghewardmills.org
Website: www.daghewardmills.org
Facebook: Dag Heward-Mills
Twitter: @EvangelistDag

ISBN ; 978-9988-596-43-9

Contents

Chapter 1

The Master Key to a Breakthrough

Now the just shall live by faith...

Hebrews 10:38

What Does It Mean to "Name It, Claim It and Take It"?

"Name it, claim it and take it", is simply a descriptive term for exercising your faith. Every Christian must have faith and must exercise it! Faith is the reason for breakthroughs and miracles in our lives. Faith is the reason for answers to prayer. Generally speaking, people who have faith are more prosperous than those who do not. I have noticed a difference between Christians who walk by faith and those who do not!

Faith people also experience disappointments, sickness and other shortcomings. However, very generally speaking, I notice a trend of blessings, abundance and long life among those who believe for them.

Now the just shall live by faith: but if any man draw back, my soul shall have no pleasure in him.

Hebrews 10:38

God is saying that if you draw away from faith, He will not be pleased with you. There are those who think that faith is not so important. They tend to draw away from the faith message and faith people. They feel that there must rather be an emphasis on patience, gentleness, holiness, etc. I believe these are important, and they all play special roles in the Christian life. This, however, does not mean we should play down on the importance of faith to the Christian life. The fact that the heart is important to the body does not mean that the kidneys are not equally important. Both are important, and both have special roles to play.

Faith is a very special virtue which has a key role to play in every Christian's life. The Bible says that without faith it is impossible to please God.

But without faith it is impossible to please him: for he that cometh to God must believe that he is, and that he is a rewarder of them that diligently seek him.

Hebrews 11:6

It is interesting to note that the Word of God does not say that without love it is impossible to please God. The Bible does not say that without peace it is impossible to please God.

The Bible is very clear on this fact: WITHOUT FAITH IT IS *IMPOSSIBLE* TO PLEASE GOD!

Abraham's faith in God was considered as an act of righteousness. Abraham believed that El' Shaddai was able to give him a child in his old age. Abraham had his faults. He lied about his wife and surrendered her twice to unbeliever kings for their pleasure.

In spite of his lying and cowardly behaviour, God was very pleased with Abraham because he had faith in His commandments.

Maybe by your standards, Abraham would have been disqualified. Perhaps in your opinion, Abraham was not a great guy. But he was a great man in God's sight. His greatness was as a result of his faith.

And being fully persuaded that, what he had promised, he was able also to perform. And therefore IT WAS IMPUTED TO HIM FOR RIGHTEOUSNESS.

Romans 4:21, 22

Dear Christian friend, God is happy, impressed and pleased when you believe in Him. When you believe that God will heal you, you make God happy! When you believe that God will prosper you, you make God excited. When you believe that your breakthrough is on the way, God is so pleased with you. When you have faith that you will live long, God is provoked to extend your life. **When you believe that God will give you increase and abundance, you excite the deep parts of El' Shaddai.** You make Him pour out the milk of His blessings into your life.

I see you walking in the great blessings of Jehovah! I see you enjoying an abundant life in God! I see you free from sickness and disease! I see the power of curses broken in your life! I see that God is pleased with you because you believe in Him!

From today, never doubt any part of God's Word. Accept that you are the champion He is speaking about. Flow with the message of prosperity, healing and abundance. Always remember that God is happy when you believe in Him.

God is not a God of poverty. Since I came to know the Lord I have not decreased in any way. I do not read about decrease, failure, setbacks and limitations in the Bible. I see only abundance, promotion and deliverance from my enemies. I see God lifting me up everyday! God did not bring you to Christ in order to demote and disgrace you. He brought you to Christ to lift and establish you in an abundant life. Jesus came that we might have life and have it more abundantly (John 10:10).

Jesus Blessed the Faith People

Under the ministry of Jesus, several people experienced personal breakthroughs. Who were they? And why did they receive these miracles?

You will remember what Jesus said about the woman with the issue of blood. This was a woman who had suffered for twelve years without any breakthrough. She came up to Jesus and received an extraordinary miracle. What was the secret of her breakthrough? Jesus gave the answer in Mark 5:3.

...Daughter, thy faith hath made thee whole...

Mark 5:34

Blind Bartimaeus received his sight miraculously. He was a noisy fellow who disturbed the service. But Jesus took notice of him and healed him. What was his secret? His secret was faith in God. He had his healing by naming it, claiming it and taking it! Look at what Jesus said to Bartimaeus:

...THY FAITH hath made thee whole.

Mark 10:52

The sinful woman who poured an alabaster box of ointment on Jesus' feet also received a miracle of forgiveness. Why did Jesus forgive her? Jesus said to the woman,

...THY FAITH hath saved thee; go in peace.

Luke 7:50

Ten lepers were healed and only one came back to say thank you. The one who came back was made whole. Why did this leper receive an extra blessing? Jesus said the same words to him.

...Arise, go thy way: THY FAITH hath made thee whole.

Luke 17:19

Two blind men came to Jesus and asked for the mercy of God. Jesus touched them and healed them. What makes such nice things happen to some people? What were His words to these two men?

...According to YOUR FAITH be it unto you.

Matthew 9:29

Have you noticed that Jesus never said, "Thy love hath made thee whole"?

Jesus never said, "Thy holiness hath saved you."

He never said, "According to your patience, be it unto you."

Why did Jesus not say, "Thy good character hath made thee whole"?

Please do not misunderstand me! I am not saying that these virtues are not important! I am saying that it is the people's faith that impressed Jesus. I am showing you that Jesus pointed out over and over that it was their faith that had brought the breakthrough. That is why the Bible says that without faith it is impossible to please God.

Have you ever thought of those men who broke through the roof of somebody's house in order to bring their paralyzed friend to Christ? Perhaps they were experienced thieves who were used to breaking into people's homes. Perhaps they were men who were used to jumping the queue and cheating others out of their rightful place. But the Bible tells us that Jesus noticed their faith and immediately responded to their needs.

And WHEN HE SAW THEIR FAITH he said unto them, Man, thy sins are forgiven thee.

Luke 5:20

Jesus didn't see their fault for jumping the queue or removing the tiles from somebody's roof. He saw their faith! Jesus sees your faith! God sees your faith! It is time for you to rise up and believe the things that are written in the Word of God. According to your faith, it shall be done unto you!

Chapter 2

Developing Real Faith

When I was a younger Christian, the concept of having faith looked far-fetched to me. After all, it seems unrealistic to command a mountain to move into the sea. Who could imagine such a thing? Even Jesus never transferred the mountains around Jerusalem to another location.

Faith has always seemed like something that emotionally strung people got involved with. It had looked like something that people who were not practical and down-to-earth got involved in. Faith people sometimes have the image of lazy Christians who are unwilling to work and just wish for good things to happen magically. But faith is none of these!

What is Faith?

Now faith is the substance of things hoped for, the evidence of things not seen.

Hebrews 11:1

Faith is the assurance of things you are hoping for. Depending on your background, faith may seem more or less substantive. If you grew up in a critical and godless society, you will have less faith in the supernatural. In spite of this, when you are born-again, you are given a measure of faith from God.

...God hath dealt to EVERY MAN the MEASURE OF FAITH.

Romans 12:3

This means that everyone has some amount of faith. You may say, "I don't believe in anything!" But that is not true! Every time you sit on a chair you are exercising faith in the chair. You believe it will not collapse, that is why you sit on it without thinking twice. Every time you sit in a car or an airplane , you are exercising faith in technology. You are also putting your faith in the driver or the pilot in the cockpit.

Whether you know it or not, you have a measure of faith. It is important to develop that faith. The subject of faith is a mysterious one and we have a lot to learn about it. I know of people who have exercised a lot of faith and this faith has resulted in many breakthroughs. There are also people who have seemingly exercised faith, without getting the same results. I do not have all the answers and neither does anyone. The Bible describes faith as a mystery.

Holding THE MYSTERY OF THE FAITH in a pure conscience.

1 Timothy 3:9

It is our duty to seek after the Lord and learn all we can from Him.

Every Christian is at a different level of faith. It is important to know that your faith can be at a higher or lower level depending on several factors. Before you can name it, claim it and take it, you must know what level of faith you are at! It is unreasonable to expect a three-year old boy to drive a real car! All he may be allowed to ride is a little tricycle, because he is just not capable of driving an adult's car!

This, however, does not make him inferior. All it means is that the boy is not mature enough to handle a real car. When he is older and mature enough, then he will be capable of handling bigger things.

There are many Christians who are believing God for things well beyond their level of faith. You must know the level of your faith. There are many things I do not pray for. There are things I have not exercised my faith about. I know I am not ready to move into certain levels of faith yet. One day when I am ready, I will. When I do exercise faith at that level, I believe I will get one hundred percent results.

Types of Faith

The Bible speaks of different levels of faith. The Word of God teaches us that you can have little faith, great faith, growing faith, dead faith, weak and strong faith and even shipwrecked faith. All these descriptive terms tell us that the status of your faith can vary.

Notice the different Scriptures that describe the levels of faith we can have.

Little Faith

...O thou of LITTLE FAITH, wherefore didst thou doubt?

Matthew 14:31

Great Faith

...I have not found so GREAT FAITH, no, not in Israel.

Matthew 8:5-10

Weak Faith

And being not WEAK IN FAITH...

Romans 4:17-19

Strong Faith

He staggered not at the promise of God; but was STRONG IN FAITH...

Romans 4:20

Exceedingly Growing Faith

We are bound to thank God always for you, brethren, as it is meet, because that your FAITH GROWETH EXCEEDINGLY...

2 Thessalonians 1:3

Increasing Faith

And the apostles said unto the Lord, INCREASE OUR FAITH.

Luke 17:5

Full of Faith

...and they chose Stephen, a man FULL OF FAITH and of the Holy Ghost...

Acts 6:5

Faith Unfeigned or Genuine Faith

Now the end of the commandment is charity out of a pure heart, and of a good conscience, and of FAITH UNFEIGNED:

1 Timothy 1:5

Unwavering Faith

But let him ask in FAITH, NOTHING WAVERING...

James 1:6

Rich Faith

...Hath not God chosen the poor of this world RICH IN FAITH...

James 2:5

Perfect or Mature Faith (Fully Developed)

Seest thou how faith wrought with his works, and by works was FAITH MADE PERFECT?

James 2:22

World Overcoming Faith

For whatsoever is born of God overcometh the world: and this is the victory that OVERCOMETH THE WORLD, EVEN OUR FAITH.

1 John 5:4

Failing Faith

But I have prayed for thee, that THY FAITH FAIL NOT...

Luke 22:32

Dead Faith

Even so FAITH, IF IT HATH NOT WORKS, IS DEAD, being alone.

James 2:17

Shipwrecked Faith

Holding faith, and a good conscience; which some having put away concerning FAITH HAVE MADE SHIPWRECK:

1 Timothy 1:19

When you look at all these types of faith, you realize that faith is a very variable condition. Do you have strong or weak faith? Are you full of faith? Is your faith dead or alive? These are important questions that you must ask yourself.

How to Improve Your Faith

You will notice that there are some types of faith that you should try not to have. Your faith must not be weak, little, dead or shipwrecked. Just as a weak or dead dog cannot guard your house, weak and dead faith can do you little good. If you are going to have a dog, get a strong one! If you are going to have faith, make sure you get living, strong and rich faith. But how does one go from little faith to great faith? How does one acquire exceedingly growing faith? What is the secret to acquiring the faith that brings breakthrough? The answer is in the Bible.

I am going to share with you Biblical methods for improving your faith. There are three simple ways to improve your faith: *hearing the right things, seeing the right things, and using it* (your faith).

Faith Comes by Hearing

The principal way to improve your faith is by hearing. The Word of God teaches us that faith comes by hearing.

So then FAITH COMETH BY HEARING, and hearing by the word of God.
Romans 10:17

Whether you like it or not, what you believe in is determined by the things you hear. There are two ways by which every human being hears or listens to things: intentionally or unintentionally. Which ever way it is, your faith ends up being affected.

Is It True?

In Ghana, certain tribes are believed to have certain characteristics. Many people believe in these characteristics, even though sometimes they have no basis for doing so. There is a tribe in Ghana which is believed to be steeped in witchcraft and juju power. One person told me that when Satan was cast out of heaven, he fell into that region of Ghana and left his slippers there!

I know of people who refuse to rent their houses to people from that tribe, no matter how much they are willing to pay. Sometimes they have not even met anyone from that particular tribe, but because these sayings have been repeated over and over, people believe that they are true. Faith comes by hearing! I find it very interesting that although there are other regions and tribes which are equally or maybe even more involved with witchcraft and occult activities, they do not receive as much attention!

My impression of people from this tribe I referred to is that they are easy going and very pleasant people. If I was to accept the things that have been said, perhaps I could not even flow with such people. I know of pastors who are even afraid to have crusades in such regions because they have heard so much about the black magic power of the region.

Perhaps they also believe that Satan fell into that region when he was cast out of heaven! You see, if such pastors had heard more about the power of God, they would probably have believed that the power of God is greater and better than any other power.

No power of the enemy can stand up to the power and the blood of Jesus.

I also know young women who are desperate for husbands, but who would prefer to remain unmarried rather than marry men from certain tribes. Why is this? They have heard over and over, that certain groups of people have certain negative characteristics.

Can You Marry a Boxer?

When I was going to get married, my wife was very hesitant to get involved with me. She had heard so many negative things from her mother and aunts who had told her that the tribe which I came from were disagreeable. They told her stories of women who had married from my tribe and were beaten up by their husbands. They went on to prove their theory by showing her that all the world famous boxers of Ghana were from that tribe!

My wife-to-be probably believed this because she had heard this from childhood. Whether you like it or not, faith comes by hearing! Even when you hear a lie, it has the power to make you believe. That is why some politicians are afraid of churches. They know that our people believe what we tell them. This is the reason why politicians try to control the media. They know that people believe what they hear, whether it is true or not.

Have you ever asked yourself why one of the first places to be captured in a military coup d'état is the broadcasting station? It is important for the new rebels to make everyone, especially the army, believe that there is a new government. The army has instructions to defend the government in power. The armed forces can only switch allegiance when they have been informed that there is a newly established government.

I once asked a Nigerian man, "What do you Nigerians think about Ghanaians?"

He immediately responded, "O we see you as people who are *poor* and *proud*!"

I thought to myself, "Perhaps this message that Ghanaians are 'poor and proud' is in the minds of many Nigerians." Maybe some have never even met any Ghanaian, yet they believe in their hearts that we are poor and very proud. Where does this notion come from? It comes from what they hear all the time.

I decided to ask several other Nigerians the same question. To my amazement, they all had the same impressions.

Where did they get these ideas from? How come they believe these things about Ghanaians? Faith comes by hearing!

What am I trying to say? All that I'm saying is that faith comes by hearing. What you keep hearing is what you believe. If you are in a church that believes in prosperity, you will believe that prosperity is a good thing and will gravitate towards it. If you are in a church which preaches that sickness and disease are sent from God to teach us humility, that is what you will believe. This is why Jesus said you must be careful about what you hear.

And he said unto them, Take heed what ye hear...

Mark 4:24

When I first became a doctor, many people said, "Now that you are a doctor you will be able to minister to people both spiritually and physically."

What people don't realize is that for seven years, I heard all about the causes, progression and the outcome of every

14

disease under the sun. Medical science teaches us that many conditions are hopeless. It teaches us how many situations are truly impossible and how the prognosis is often bleak.

After hearing such things for years, it is an uphill task to believe that God can and will undo the sicknesses that ravage the human race. I find it far easier to have faith when I don't know the medical implications of a thing.

Faith comes by hearing. You must be careful about what you hear.

Guard Your Ears

If you hear that the economy is going down and therefore everyone is going down, you will believe and act accordingly. Money, which is a piece of paper, depends on the faith of the masses. As soon as the faith of people in money or in the banking system drops, the whole financial world can collapse. Whenever there is bad news in some major financial center, it sends ripples of fear into the minds of the millionaires of this world. They begin to scramble for their money. This is what causes stock markets and banks to go crashing down.

We must learn how important it is to guard our ears. You must not allow yourself to hear bad news and discouraging stories. Fear is a type of faith and it also comes by hearing. You must select your friends and walk with people who speak encouraging and positive words.

I once had some friends who didn't believe in me. They criticized me all the time. They saw no good thing in my ministry. I got rid of all those people and now I am surrounded by friends who say positive things.

It is also important for you to speak positively over your children. If you tell them, "You are daft", "You are stupid" and "You are bad", they will soon believe that they are daft, stupid and bad. I know of children who have been called "devil" by relatives until they eventually turned out to be human "devils".

This is why listening to tapes is such an important spiritual exercise. You must intentionally acquire preaching tapes and soak them in.

You must not listen to worldly music. You must surround yourself with Christian music. Music has a message and you will soon believe what you are hearing.

Faith Is Affected by What You See

Although this statement is not in the Bible, it is also true. What is not explicit in scripture is often implicit in the Word! When Peter walked on the water, he did very well and his faith worked perfectly until he saw certain things.

BUT WHEN HE SAW the wind boisterous, he was afraid; and beginning to sink, he cried, saying, Lord, save me.

Matthew 14:30

He saw the wind and the waves and this had a terrible effect on his faith. What you see affects your faith! Peter's faith dropped drastically and he began to sink. Peter did not hear a message of doubt to disturb his faith level. He was not told anything to fill his heart with doubt. He just saw the wrong things! He saw the wind and the waves in action and that is what struck at his faith.

It is sometimes better to pray and believe God about things without seeing certain things. When you begin to observe the wind, waves and the water, your faith can fly out of the window!

Faith Comes by Using It

Everyone has a level of faith. The more you use it, the more it increases. If you believe God for a bicycle and it happens, your faith will rise and you will have faith to believe God for a car. It is like lifting weights. You start from a lighter object and graduate upwards.

Jesus told the parable of the nobleman who gave a pound each to his ten servants. On his return from a long journey, he inquired from each of them how much they had gained by trading (using). You will discover from this parable that using of the one pound led to a natural increase in the number of pounds.

He said therefore, A certain nobleman went into a far country to receive for himself a kingdom, and to return.

And he called his ten servants, and delivered them ten pounds, and said unto them, Occupy till I come.

But his citizens hated him, and sent a message after him, saying, We will not have this man to reign over us.

And it came to pass, that when he was returned, having received the kingdom, then he commanded these servants to be called unto him, to whom he had given the money, that he might know how much every man had GAINED BY TRADING.

Then came the first, saying, Lord thy pound hath gained ten pounds.

And he said unto him, Well done, thou good servant: because thou hast been faithful in very little, have thou authority over ten cities.

Luke 19:12-17

I find it easier to pray for the sick now. Sometime ago it was difficult to exercise my faith in that area of ministry. After doing it for some time, it takes less effort to believe God for miracles of healing in miracle services. Faith definitely increases as you use it. God has given us the principle of gaining by trading. You gain as you trade! You increase as you use it!

As you use these three principles, your faith will gradually move from weak to strong and from little to great! You will no longer have dead or shipwrecked faith. As you hear testimonies of great things that God has done, your faith for the same will rise. Your faith will become exceedingly growing faith.

Chapter 3

Name It!

What do you want from God? Just name it! I have discovered that God is our greatest friend. Traditionally, people have blamed the Lord for every bad thing that happened. Even in legal jargon, events like earthquakes, floods and tornadoes are called "Acts of God". What does this mean? What are they trying to say? They are blaming God for the bad things which occur! What about the devil? If God does all these evil things, what does the devil spend his time doing?

Whenever something bad happens, people would say, "God is moving in a mysterious way, His wonders to perform." In a certain sense, it is true that God is mysterious to us but, His real nature is revealed in the Word.

In Genesis chapter 1, God is known as "Elohim", the Creator of the universe and the Creator of nature. In the life of Abraham, God reveals Himself as "El'Shaddai". "El'Shaddai" is the God who goes against nature and blesses Abraham with a child in his old age. We see Him as the one who blesses His children giving them long life and prosperity.

How then do we blame Him for every bad thing that happens? The devil wants you to believe that God is fighting against you. The opposite is true! God is the best friend you have. The God you serve is the God of promotion and blessing. If God did not hold back Jesus Christ, what good thing will He withhold from us? He that spared not his own Son, but delivered him up for us all, how shall he not with him also freely give us all things?

Romans 8:32

The Bible describes God as the sun and the shield who gives grace and glory. God is giving you beauty for ashes right now! He's making your life glorious as you name it and claim it!

For the Lord God is a sun and shield: the Lord will give grace and glory: no good thing will he withhold from them that walk uprightly.

Psalm 84:11

Did God Try to Kill Jesus?

I want you to remember an experience that the disciples had with the Lord. They were in a boat trying to cross the Sea of Galilee when a storm struck. What did Jesus do?

Did he stand up and declare, *"God moves in a mysterious way his wonders to perform"*?

Did he say, *"I don't know why God has sent this storm to kill me, but He is working His perfect plan"*?

No, he did not! He rebuked the storm.

...Then he arose, and REBUKED the wind and the raging of the water: and they ceased, and there was a great calm.

Luke 8:24

If God is the one who sent the storm to kill Jesus and the disciples, then Jesus actually rebuked God. By rebuking the storm, Jesus was disapproving of it. He was stopping the agents of destruction from shortening his life and ministry. Did Jesus rebuke God? Certainly not! The storm was not an "Act of God" sent to destroy them!

The Bible teaches us that it is the thief or the devil who comes to steal, to kill and to destroy.

The thief cometh not, but for to steal, and to kill, and to destroy: I am come that they might have life, and that they might have it more abundantly.

John 10:10

God does not come into your life to destroy you! El'Shaddai does not come into your life to kill you. He is here right now to prolong your life and to extend your days. Your duty is to know and to believe that God is your friend who is trying to help you. In actual fact, God is your very best friend.

...and there is a friend that sticketh closer than a brother.

Proverbs 18:24

The devil is the one who is trying to disgrace and destroy you! Satan is the one who has set limitations and barriers all around you. But today, as you rise up in faith to name it, claim it and take it, I see your enemies perish!

Because God is such a good God, He wants you to name your blessings. Traditionally, we have thought that having nice things is sinful. To be a holy Christian means to be nothing and to have nothing. But God has a bountiful store of blessings waiting for those that believe. That is why His Word says you can ask for whatsoever you desire and you can receive it.

Therefore I say unto you, What things soever ye desire, when ye pray, believe that ye receive them, and ye shall have them.

Mark 11:24

This Scripture does not say, "Whatsoever things you *need.*" It does not say, "Whatsoever things *God desires for you.*" It says, "Whatsoever *YOU* desire."

Please read it loud and clear! God is saying that you can have *your* desires. What do *you* desire? What is your wish? God wants you to name it! God wants you to ask for it! **The reason why many Christians do not have answers to their prayers is**

because they do not ask. Often we think we are carnal if we ask for nice things. But the Bible is very clear on this.

... ye have not, because ye ask not.

James 4:2

If God did not withhold Jesus Christ from us, what good thing is He going to keep back from your life? (Romans 8:32)

One of the Scriptures I love is John 15:7.

If ye abide in me, and my words abide in you, ye shall ask what ye will, and it shall be done unto you.

John 15:7

Jesus was teaching us that God is prepared to give us what we want. He said that you shall ask what you will and not what God wills for you. God knows that you have a will. You can choose to serve Him or not! God wants to work with people who have chosen to and are willing to serve Him.

The fact that you are a Christian does not mean that you no longer have a will or a desire for certain things. God knows that and He encourages you to come to Him and ask for what you wish. This is the Word of God.

Of course, there are some conditions. John 15:7 says that if you abide in Him and His Word abides in you, you can ask for what you want! **When you abide in Christ your desires will line up with the Word of God.** I came to know the Lord years ago. My desire now is to win more people to Christ. I desire to experience church growth and the blessings of the Holy Spirit.

Somebody may ask, "Don't you desire more money or cars?" The answer is no. If it was money I desired, I would simply practice medicine in America. That would be a simpler way of satisfying a desire for money.

The problem many people have is that they think it is impossible to have more spiritual desires than carnal ones. It is not! There is a certain level of spiritual maturity where carnal things do not mean so much to you.

As you abide in Christ and His Word abides in you, you will desire things that are consistent with the Word of God. When you name them and claim them, you will receive them.

When you have the right heart, wealth and riches cannot destroy you. All the patriarchs who served the Lord were blessed with abundance and wealth. The prosperity of Abraham, Isaac and Jacob often intimidated their neighbors and incited jealousy. The Bible says that Abraham was very rich. God had made him rich. In fact, at one time, Abraham wanted people around to know that it was not them who had contributed to his riches. Because of this he refused a large gift from the King of Sodom.

> **And Abram said to the king of Sodom, I have lift up mine hand unto the Lord, the most high God, the possessor of heaven and earth. That I will not take from a thread even to a shoe latchet, and that I will not take anything that is thine, lest thou shouldest say, I have made Abram rich:**
>
> **Genesis 14:22, 23**

God was obviously prospering Abraham. Abraham knew that his prosperity was coming from one source - El' Shaddai. Remember that every good and perfect gift comes from above. Abraham's faith in God was not destroyed by his riches. The Bible makes it clear that it is the love of money and not money itself that corrupts.

> **For THE LOVE of money is the root of all evil...**
>
> **1 Timothy 6:10**

From today, begin to name all the things that you desire from your heavenly Father. He is standing by to respond to your faith. *Don't forget that God is impressed with people who believe in Him.*

Chapter 4

Claim It!

To "claim it" means to confess your faith about what you desire from the Lord. Traditionally, confession has always revolved around the subject of sin. However, it is important for us to know that there are five types of biblical confessions and not just one.

Five Types of Confessions

Confessing Your Sins to the Father

The first type of confession is a confession of sin to the Father. This is the well-known type of biblical confession. **It is important for Christians to confess their sins to God on a regular basis.** The Bible tells us that if we think we have no sin we deceive ourselves and the truth is not in us. None of us is without sin.

No matter how hard you try, sin is part of our flesh and our minds. That is why the scripture says if we say we have no sins we are actually deceiving ourselves.

> **If we say that we have no sin, we deceive ourselves, and the truth is not in us. If we confess our sins, he is faithful and just to forgive us our sins, and to cleanse us from all unrighteousness.**
>
> **1 John 1:8, 9**

It is a dangerous thing to think that you are sinless by your own strength.

Commission and Omission

There are three types of sins: the sins of commission, the sins of omission and the sins of the heart. **Sins of commission are the things you actually do.** Those sins are easy to recognize and therefore easy to confess. When you have a negative thought, you definitely know that you have had a negative thought. It is easy to recognize and to confess this to God.

Sins of omission are the things we don't do. They are things we are supposed to do that we don't do.

> **Therefore for him that knoweth to do good, and doeth it not, to him it is sin.**
>
> **James 4:17**

Maybe God wants you to win somebody to Christ and you fail to speak out. That is a sin of omission. Perhaps God wanted you to pray and you failed to pray. Perhaps God wanted you to support His work financially and you didn't do it. You may not even be aware of the fact that you are sinning. That is why you need to confess your sins on a regular basis.

Heart Sins

Sins of the heart are even more difficult to recognize. What we often do not recognize is that the heart of man is a very deep thing. There are times when your heart is full of evil and you are not even aware of it. That is why the psalmist cried out, "Search me, O God, and know my heart..." David wanted God to take evil things away from his heart. Sometimes our hearts are full of pride and rebellion and we do not even know it. But God looks at the heart.

> **For the Lord seeth not as man seeth; man looketh on the outward appearance, but THE LORD LOOKETH ON THE HEART.**
>
> **1 Samuel 16:7**

25

The cry of the psalmist is an important prayer for us all.

Search me, O God, and know my heart: try me, and know my thoughts: And see if there be any wicked way in me, and lead me in the way everlasting.

Psalm 139:23, 24

Why did King David want God to look into his heart? Couldn't David see whether there was something wicked in his heart? Perhaps not! We sometimes do not even know ourselves. No one knows Toyota like the people who make Toyota. No one knows Ford like the people who make Ford cars. No one knows you like the God who made you. The creator knows the creature better than anyone else!

Confessing Your Faults One to Another

The second type of confession is the confession of faults one to another. Although confession of sins to the Father results in forgiveness, there are times it is necessary to speak to someone else about the problem you have. Confessing your faults to someone else is not done in order to receive forgiveness. Forgiveness is received from the Father when you confess your sins.

There are times when we need healing and restoration within our spirit. Talking about these things and confessing them out loud helps to heal and eventually overcome the psychological wounds that are acquired through sin.

The King James Version of James 5:16 says, "Confess your faults one to another... that ye may be healed..." The Amplified Bible throws more light on this same scripture.

CONFESS TO ONE ANOTHER therefore your faults (your slips, your false steps, your offenses, your sins) and pray also for one another, THAT YOU MAY BE *HEALED AND RESTORED* (TO A SPIRITUAL TONE OF MIND AND HEART)...

James 5:16 (Amplified Translation)

We all need to be restored to a spiritual tone of heart and mind. When you have made a mistake, you need restoration. Restoration comes through confessing to one another. Of course telling your problem to the wrong person will only lead to complications.

I have noticed that people experience permanent healing and restoration through this second type of confession.

Confessing Christ for Salvation

The third important type of confession is the confession of our faith in Jesus in order to receive salvation.

If thou shalt CONFESS WITH THY MOUTH the Lord Jesus, and shalt believe in thine heart that God hath raised him from the dead, thou shalt be saved.

Romans 10:9

Contrary to traditional opinion, it is not the confession of sins that leads to salvation, but a confession of Christ as your Lord and Saviour. **It is important to confess your sins and repent genuinely, but the Bible makes it clear that it is the confession of Jesus Christ as Lord and Savior that leads to the salvation of the soul.**

Whenever you lead someone to Christ, in addition to whatever you say, ensure that the person is led to confess Jesus Christ as Lord and Saviour.

Confession of our Faith

Let us hold fast the profession [confession] of our faith without wavering...

Hebrews 10:23

The word translated profession in the King James Bible comes from the Greek word, *homologia*. This word means "to agree". It is sometimes translated "profession" or "confession".

As a Christian body, there are things that constitute the essentials of our faith. Our Christian faith can be confessed or professed. We can speak out and declare what our essential beliefs are. What we call the Apostles' Creed is a good example of the confession of our faith. It is a good thing to say because it constitutes the essentials of what Christians believe. Virtually every line of this creed has a deep meaning.

The Apostles' Creed

I believe in God the Father Almighty, Maker of Heaven and Earth;

And in Jesus Christ His only Son our Lord, who was conceived by the Holy Ghost; born of the Virgin Mary; suffered under Pontius Pilate, was crucified, dead, and buried; He descended into hell; the third day He rose again from the dead; He ascended into Heaven, and sitteth at the right hand of God, the Father Almighty; from there He shall come to judge the quick and the dead.

I believe in the Holy Spirit; the Holy Catholic (universal) Church; the Communion of saints; the forgiveness of sins; the resurrection of the body, and life everlasting. Amen.

You will notice that we believe that Jesus was born of a virgin and not just of a "young woman" as some are claiming today. There is a difference between a virgin and a "young woman"!

This confession also states that Jesus suffered under Pontius Pilate.

Pontius Pilate is the only other person whose name is mentioned in this statement. He tried to wash the murder of Jesus off his hands but the church did not allow him to do so. That is why his name is mentioned here. We will never forget how he had Jesus killed!

This reminds me of some authorities today. They behave just like Pontius Pilate and refuse to do the right thing. They also cannot wash their hands! One day when the history books are

being written, it will be stated that the church su...
hands of such people. Dear friend, beware, you car...
your hands!

This confession also speaks of Jesus rising from...
faith rests on this great fact of history. It is this an... ...., ... ract
of his resurrection that separates Christ from every other religious
leader. The tomb is empty! There is no place which is as revered
as the tomb of Christ. His followers knew that He rose from that
place!

Another interesting part of this confession is that Jesus will
return to judge the living and the dead. When we say this
confession, we remind ourselves of the coming judgement. We
remind ourselves of the day of accountability. We declare that
Jesus will return from the skies to judge people. Such a thing
sounds crazy! Only mad people would believe something like that,
some may say. But that is the Christian's faith! And when we say
these things, we affirm our faith.

Finally, we declare that we believe in the church and in the
communion (fellowship) of saints. We believe in spending our time
in fellowship with other Christians.

We confess that we are glad to go to church. We enjoy the
company of other Christians.

This is the confession of our faith. We must say it to remind
ourselves of what we really believe. When we declare our faith, it
becomes real to us.

God wants us to say things that agree with our faith. **Our words
must confirm specific things we believe in our heart.** Claiming
what you believe shows that you have the spirit of faith at work in
your life! When a person has a spirit of drunkenness, he drinks a
lot and is often drunk. When a person has a spirit of immorality, he
gets involved in immoral acts. When a person has a spirit of faith,
he confesses positive things that he believes in.

Ve having the same SPIRIT OF FAITH, according as it is written, I believed and therefore have I spoken; WE ALSO BELIEVE AND THEREFORE SPEAK.

2 Corinthians 4:13

Confession of Specific Faith

Remember that you take your place in Christ and in Heaven by making a confession. You will also take your place in this life by confessing boldly the things that you desire from the Lord. It is time to rise up and claim them. It is time to rise up and speak them out. Declare that you will live long. Declare that you are unbeatable and unquenchable by the devil. Declare that you are undefeatable, "undiminishable", "unmolestable" and "undieable" before the age of seventy!

What do you lose by speaking out boldly? Instead of allowing thoughts of fear and panic to ravage your mind, declare that Satan cannot disgrace or limit you in this life. Declare that you are healthy, blessed, prosperous and rich!

What do you have to lose? Open your mouth and declare that your enemies are disgraced and disappointed! Proclaim that God has given you beauty for ashes. Your life is beautiful from today! Your marriage and business are beautiful from today! Declare that beauty characterizes everything you do! Take no notice of the frightening events all around you. If a thousand seem to be falling on your left and ten thousand on your right, declare that it will not happen to you. You have nothing to lose by declaring your faith. Speak it out for that is the spirit of faith at work!

How to Monitor Your Faith Level

The claims you make in life are what we use to assess your level of faith. The Bible says that because you believe you speak. That means that your claims are a direct result of your faith level. If you want to assess yourself, listen to your proclamations and declarations. The bigger your claims the bigger your faith. **Great faith brings forth great declarations!**

It is time to speak about living long! It is time to speak about healing power! It is time to declare how God has prospered you by faith! It is time to declare that you are fruitful in the vineyard of the Lord! Claim your place among God's generals!

Claim your place in God's glorious army! Declare that you are one of the righteous trees planted by the Lord! Do not be afraid of falling. Declare that you will stand and not fall!

You Can Have What You Say

Can you really have what you say? The answer is yes! You are actually experiencing what you have said with your mouth. Mark 11:23-24 tells us that mountains will respond to what you say. Begin to say big things, because you have a big God. Say them consistently! That is how you make your claim. It is time to name it, claim it and take it! Take no notice of the doubters. There will always be an opposition party. There will always be a commentator.

Notice how many times the word "say" appears in this verse.

For verily I say unto you, That whosoever shall say unto this mountain, Be thou removed, and be thou cast into the sea; and shall not doubt in his heart, but shall believe that those things which he saith shall come to pass, he shall have whatsoever he saith. Therefore I say unto you, What things soever ye desire, when ye pray, believe that ye receive them, and ye shall have them.

Mark 11:23,24

It appears five times. God is telling you that you will have what you say. The promise is not that you will have what you think! This verse is not promising that you will have what you hope for, it is promising that you will have what you say!

Enter in like a little child right now and receive great breakthroughs by claiming your blessings. You are what you say you are! And you can do what you say you can do! You are beautiful because God has made you so! You are successful because you say so! You are intelligent and wise because that is what you are claiming to be!

"Oh pastor, is it that simple?" It is as simple as you make it to be!

You cannot experience any of the blessings of the kingdom of God unless you enter in like a little child. If you live in Africa, you will find yourself surrounded by many unsolvable problems. There are many hopeless situations in this great continent. Today, I am offering you an answer which is not found through governments or politicians. The master key to your blessing is to name it, claim it and take it!

Paul said that he could do all things through Christ. I also believe that I can do all things through Christ who strengthens me. Never say, "I cannot do it!" You will have what you say. You will experience the things that you say. I am not telling you to be unrealistic, I am telling you to exercise faith. I am a very realistic person, but I am continually exercising my faith. **It is important to balance the handling of certain realities with the exercising of faith.**

You may have to take medicine in order to stay alive. That does not mean you do not have faith. You can exercise your faith as you take that medication, by constantly declaring your faith and victory over disease and sickness. Remember; you will have what you say.

Apostle Paul was the greatest teacher of faith, yet he was also a practical man. He advised Timothy not to drink water but to use a little wine for his stomach and other diseases.

Drink no longer water, but use a little wine for thy stomach's sake and thine often infirmities.

1 Timothy 5:23

Tongue Power!

Did you know that there is power in your tongue? And no ordinary power at that! The power of life and death is found in the tongue:

Death and life are in the power of the tongue: and they that love it shall eat the fruit thereof.

Proverbs 18:21

You must tap into this great power of the tongue by naming it and claming it! Claim your victory over darkness. Pronounce your deliverance from the spirits of inferiority and self-pity! You can do all things through Christ who strengthens you! Declare that you have overcome the demons of worry and anxiety! You are free from nervousness and headaches! Depression and madness have no power over your life!

I see you having favour in all that you do! **The power for abundance and wealth rests in your ability to claim it!** It is time to rise up and pronounce yourself free from cancer and disease. Claim a healthy and long life, in the name of Jesus. You are free from genetic and demonic curses.

Conversations and Commands

The power to live on is in your tongue. There are two types of confessions or claims: *conversational confessions (claims) and commanding confessions (claims).*

You must be careful with what you say, even in casual conversation. Often it is in casual conversation that you declare the things that you really believe. At other times you can make deliberate commanding confessions. During these commanding claims, you lay hold on victories and breakthroughs by conscious and deliberate confessions. Both of these types of confessions (conversational and commanding) have power.

A trap is a trap! Whether you put your foot in the trap intentionally or unintentionally does not matter. The trap will still function and grip your leg. You must know from today that your words will trap (snare) you whether you spoke intentionally or unintentionally.

Thou art snared with the words of thy mouth, thou art taken with the words of thy mouth.

Proverbs 6:2

I remember how a distant relation would jokingly speak about a pimple on his face. He would point to the pimple and say, "This is my cancer". Obviously, he had no intention of acquiring cancer on his face. A few years later this same man developed a cancer on his face and eventually died of it.

You are trapped by the words that you speak. Don't say things you don't mean.

Out of the same mouth proceedeth blessing and cursing. My brethren, these things ought not so to be.

James 3:10

I know that most people think that the tongue is a small and insignificant member of the body. However, you must realize that it is like the power of a small rudder that controls huge ships.

I have ridden strong African racehorses. These horses often had the power and strength to run for miles at very high speeds. Yet, I was able to control these mighty horses by means of small bits in their mouths.

Your life is an important and complex thing, but it can be controlled by your tongue. Declare that your blessings are permanent! Claim your promotion in this life, in the name of Jesus! Openly thank the Lord that no weapon formed against you will prosper! Declare that you are marching on! I see you marching on and the gates of hell cannot stop you! I see you free from the power of sin, shame and disgrace!

It's Time to Frame Your World

Through faith we understand that the worlds were framed by the word of God, so that things which are seen were not made of things which do appear

Hebrews 11:3

Some people wonder how this world came into existence. Stop searching and read the Bible. God made the world through the power of the spoken Word. He simply said, "Let there be..." and there was! He spoke the world into existence by simple and powerful pronouncements. "Let there be light..." and there was light!

And God said, Let the waters bring forth abundantly...

Genesis 1:20

When God spoke to the waters to be fruitful, the waters had no choice but to be fruitful. God wants us to imitate Him. Ephesians 5:1 tells us to be imitators of God. That means that we must be holy, because God is holy. That means we must be righteous, because we are imitating a righteous God. **It also means that we are to frame our world by making declarations.**

Let there be happiness in my home! Let there be abundance of all things in my life! Let my cup run over! Let my children live long and prosper! Let my body be healthy and live long! Let my enemies be blown away like the chaff of the wind! Let those that hate me wither and fade away! Let the crooked paths in my life be straightened! Let poverty run away from my home! Let righteousness characterize my life! Let holiness be part of my life from today! Let me be fruitful! Let me be pleasing to God in all that I do!

Be an imitator of God in this aspect of commanding, claiming, announcing and insisting on your blessings! Begin to imitate your Heavenly Father by affirming, declaring, demanding, maintaining, asserting and pronouncing your breakthrough. That is the God-kind of faith.

35

Did you know that you can speak to things that do not have physical ears and they will respond?

Jesus did that all the time. He once spoke to a fig tree and said,

No man eat fruit of thee hereafter for ever.

Mark 11:14

Jesus spoke to the wind and the sea. Does the sea have ears? The answer is no, but it can respond to your commands of faith!

And he arose, and rebuked the wind, AND SAID UNTO THE SEA, Peace, be still. And the wind ceased, and there was a great calm.

Mark 4:39

One time Jesus even spoke to a dead body. He commanded the dead person to listen. Jesus interrupted the funeral procession and raised a young man back to life in the city of Naim.

And he came and touched the bier [coffin]; and they that bare him stood still. And he said, YOUNG MAN, I SAY UNTO THEE, ARISE. And he that was dead sat up...

Luke 7:14,15

I see you commanding your dead business to resurrect! Declare over your shop the victory of Jehovah! Speak to your bank account and tell it to come alive! Announce to every mountain facing you that it will have to move! Affirm the fact that every impossible situation will be made possible! Insist that you have the victory everyday, in spite of what you see or feel! We walk by faith and not by sight!

For we walk by faith, not by sight:

2 Corinthians 5:7

Naming it and claiming it, is not the same as seeing and feeling things. We do not live by our feelings. Feelings are real, but God has not asked us to live by them. We are to live by our faith. The father of faith, Abraham, believed that he would have a child. In spite of how he felt, he called those things that were not, as though they were!

(As it is written, I have made thee a father of many nations,) before him whom he believed, even God, who quickeneth the dead, and CALLETH THOSE THINGS WHICH BE NOT AS THOUGH THEY WERE.

Romans 4:17

I know that there are many things that do not seem realistic. God is not asking you to be realistic; He is asking you to walk by your faith. God is telling you to believe in His Word. You will never be the same after you apply these laws to your life.

In this next section, I want to share with you some biblical things that you should name and claim.

Chapter 5

I Am! I Have! I Can!

When it comes to naming and claiming, the most important thing for you to do is to stay with the Word of God. God will not back foolish and childish claims. Your earthly father would take no notice of you if you claimed certain unrealistic and impractical things. If you spend time confessing foolish imaginations, even the devil will take no notice of you!

You are NOT the Queen of England so there is no use for you to spend time confessing that! I am NOT the Prince of Wales and there is no need for me to claim that! God has not told me in His Word that He wants me to be an astronaut; I do not confess unrealistic things that will not happen! Neither should you! Once you stay with the Word of God you are on safe ground.

> **...I say unto you, The Son can do nothing of himself, but what he seeth the Father do: for what things soever he doeth, these also doeth the Son likewise.**
>
> **John 5:19**

There are three things that you can confess with safety. You can confess what you are in Christ, what you have in Christ and what you can do in Christ.

Let us run through a few of the things that are clearly stated in the Word of God. I want you to affirm and attest to the fact that you are what the Bible says you are. I want you to declare that you can do what the Bible says you can do. I want you to insist to all and sundry that you have what you say the Bible says you have.

I AM

I Am Born-Again

That if thou shalt confess with thy mouth the Lord Jesus, and shalt believe in thine heart that God hath raised him from the dead, **THOU SHALT BE SAVED** [born again].

Romans 10:9

I Am a New Creature

Therefore if any man be in Christ, **HE IS A NEW CREATURE:** old things are passed away; behold, all things are become new.

2 Corinthians 5:17

I Am Complete

For in him dwelleth all the fulness of the God-head bodily. And **YE ARE COMPLETE** in him, which is the head of all principality and power.

Colossians 2:9,10

I Am Delivered

Who hath **DELIVERED US** from the power of darkness, and hath translated us into the kingdom of his dear son:

Colossians 1:13

I Am Free

Stand fast therefore in the liberty wherewith **CHRIST HATH MADE US FREE...**

Galatians 5:1

I Am Blessed

Blessed be the God and Father of our Lord Jesus Christ, WHO HATH BLESSED US with all spiritual blessings in heavenly places in Christ:

Ephesians 1:3

According as HIS DIVINE POWER HATH GIVEN UNTO US ALL THINGS that pertain unto life and godliness, through the knowledge of him that hath called us to glory and virtue:

2 Peter 1:3

I Am An Heir

...Wherefore thou art no more a servant, but a son; and if a son, then AN HEIR OF GOD through Christ.

Galatians 4:6,7

I Am a King

AND HATH MADE US KINGS and priests unto God and his Father...

Revelations 1:6

I Am the Righteousness of God

For he hath made him to be sin for us, who knew no sin; THAT WE MIGHT BE MADE THE RIGHTEOUSNESS OF GOD in him.

2 Corinthians 5:21

Based on these Scriptures you have a right to make these claims. I tell you, your faith will become effective and powerful as you confess these things which are in line with the Word of God.

Many Christians want to know how to have faith that works. Faith that works is the faith that makes confessions. The faith that is effective is the faith that vocalizes its claims. It is not enough to think or dream, you must speak out! This is an eternal principle of the Word of God.

Notice this amazing Scripture in the book of Philemon.

That the communication of thy FAITH MAY BECOME EFFECTUAL by the acknowledging of every good thing which is in you in Christ Jesus.

Philemon 6

Faith becomes effective when you acknowledge and affirm the good things that are in you because of Christ.

I HAVE

I Have All Things

According as his divine power hath given unto us ALL THINGS that pertain unto life and godliness, through the knowledge of him that hath called us to glory and virtue:

2 Peter 1:3

I Have Dominion

And God said, Let us make man in our image, after our likeness: and let them have DOMINION...

Genesis 1:26

I Have the Desires of My Heart

Delight thyself also in the Lord; and HE SHALL GIVE THEE THE DESIRES OF THINE HEART.

Psalm 37:4

I Have the Spirit of Power, Love and a Sound Mind

For God hath not given us the spirit of fear; but of POWER, and of LOVE, and of A SOUND MIND.

2 Timothy 1:7

I Have the Blessings of Abraham

Christ hath redeemed us from the curse of the law, being made a curse for us: for it is written, Cursed is every one that hangeth on a tree: THAT THE BLESSING OF ABRAHAM MIGHT COME ON THE GENTILES, through Jesus Christ; that we might receive the promise of the Spirit through faith.

Galatians 3:13, 14

I Have the Greater One In Me

...GREATER IS HE THAT IS IN YOU, than he that is in the world.

1 John 4:4

I Have the Power of God Working through Me

But unto them which are called, both Jews and Greeks, Christ THE POWER OF GOD, and the wisdom of God.

1 Corinthians 1:24

I Have the Wisdom of Christ Operating through Me

But unto them which are called, both Jews and Greeks, Christ the power of God, and THE WISDOM OF GOD. But of him are ye in Christ Jesus, who of God is made unto us WISDOM...

1 Corinthians 1:24, 30

The Scriptures you are reading are the legal and scriptural basis for making these confessions. **You can declare these things over and over because they are Bible-based.** These are not the words of an irresponsible dreamer. These are the words of a faith-filled Christian.

In Luke 7, when Jesus encountered the centurion whose servant was ill he marvelled at the great faith of this centurion. The centurion said, "Do not come to my house. Just stand where you are and say something"!

He said to Jesus, "Speak in a word and my servant will be healed." The man had confidence in the spoken Word of God. Thank God for things that are written but it's time now to speak. It's time now to name it and claim it!

I CAN

I Can Do All Things!

I CAN DO ALL THINGS through Christ which strengtheneth me.

Philippians 4:13

I Can Reign In life!

...they which receive abundance of grace and of the gift of righteousness shall reign in life by one, Jesus Christ.

Romans 5:17

I Can Do Greater Works Than Jesus Did!

Verily, verily, I say unto you, He that believeth on me, the works that I do shall he do also; AND GREATER WORKS THAN THESE SHALL HE DO; because I go unto my Father.

John 14:12

I Can Cast Out Devils!

And these signs shall follow them that believe; In my name SHALL THEY CAST OUT DEVILS...

Mark 16:17

I Can Heal the Sick!

And these signs shall follow them that believe... THEY SHALL LAY HANDS ON THE SICK, AND THEY SHALL RECOVER.

Mark 16:17

I Can Overcome This Mountain!

For whatsoever is born of God OVERCOMETH THE WORLD: and this is the victory that overcometh the world, even our faith.

1 John 5:4

I Can Make It!

For whatsoever is born of God overcometh the world: and THIS IS THE VICTORY that overcometh the world, even our faith.

1 John 5:4

Paul prayed for the Ephesian Christians, that the Lord would open their eyes to see the riches of their inheritance. In other words, God wants His children to see how rich an inheritance He has given to them. From today, I want you to see your rich inheritance! I want you to accept that all these things are real! Say them over and over again.

There are some people who think the faith message is past. You are making a big mistake if you try to leave out faith. Jesus said, "These things ought you to do, not neglecting the others."(Matthew 23:23)

Is the Faith Message Outmoded?

Whenever Christians find a new message, they often neglect the earlier message. If you leave out faith, you will find yourself coming back to pick it up. There can be no victorious Christian life without faith. I speak positive confessions about my life everyday. I confess boldly about how fruitful I am in the kingdom.

That is what I am believing God for and that is what I am seeing.

I see you rising up into your blessing now! I see you becoming more Christ-like and more glorious! You are what God says you are! You are not a failure! You are not a disgrace! There is no shame in your life!

God has lifted you up and promoted you! Your enemies shall be blown away like the chaff of the wind! I see God increasing you! Everything you touch is blessed! I see your business flourishing! I see your family flourishing! Your prosperity has become like the dust of the earth! Your blessings have become like the stars in the sky! Your great increase has become like the sand on the sea shore!

You are no ordinary person! You are a champion! You are a true champion! You can win! God is strengthening your right hand to conquer the enemy! Do not be afraid from today, the devil is the one who is frightened! Rise up and speak over the church you are pastoring! Speak to the empty chairs and tell them to be filled! You are anointed! You are full and not empty!

Command your intelligence to respond to your confessions! Command your decisions to line up to the positive claims you are making! You can win! You are indeed a successful person!

I see you with Solomonic and Davidic success! Enjoy the blessings of El' Shaddai! The blessings of the breast are your portion! You will have no need from today because the Lord has heard your cry!

Declare that you have one hundred percent answers to your prayers. Declare that you are a good husband or wife. Maintain your confession that quarrels are not part of your marriage.

Speak over your children. Call them blessed. Call them angels. Call them anointed! Declare over your old car: you are new and a blessing to me!

I see God opening your ears now! You will hear from God every time you pray! You have answers to your prayers!

God has given you insight and revelation. All your decisions are characterized by wisdom and intelligence. Greater is He that is in you, than he that is in the world!

Chapter 6

How to Take It!

Be strong and of a good courage: for unto this people shalt thou divide for an inheritance the land, which I sware unto their fathers to give them. This book of the law shall not depart out of thy mouth; but thou shalt meditate therein day and night, that thou mayest observe to do according to all that is written therein: for then thou shalt make thy way prosperous, and then thou shalt have good success.

Joshua 1:6, 8

Joshua was the army general who took the Promised Land. If you want to walk into your possession, study the life of Joshua and follow his example.

Joshua was told to be strong and very courageous. He was also told to meditate on the Word of God. All these were to enable him to obey the Word of God. To "take your claims", means to act on the Word of God. It means to act on your faith and thereby possess your possession.

It takes courage to act on your faith. That is why God told Joshua to be strong and very courageous. It takes courage to do an altar call.

It takes courage to pray for the sick. What about if no one is healed? That is where courage comes in.

If you want financial prosperity, you must obey the Word of God, which tells us to work hard.

Galatians 6:7 teaches us that we reap whatever we sow. Whatever you put in, you will reap either a thirty fold, a sixty fold, or a hundred fold.

Be not deceived; God is not mocked: for whatsoever a man soweth, that shall he also reap.

Galatians 6:7

Proverbs 6:6-8 tells us that ants are prosperous.

Go to the ant, thou sluggard; consider her ways, and be wise: which having no guide, overseer, or ruler, provideth her meat in the summer, and gathereth her food in the harvest.

Proverbs 6:6-8

They mind their own business and work without supervision. If you really want the financial prosperity that you are confessing, then you must decide to work without supervision - like the ant. Do you want to experience a financial breakthrough? It is not enough just to confess great things. You must obey the Word of God.

You must obey the Word of God which instructs you to give your tithes and offerings regularly.

Upon the first day of the week let every one of you lay by him in store, as God hath prospered him, that there be no gatherings when I come.

1 Corinthians 16:2

BRING YE ALL THE TITHES into the storehouse, that there may be meat in mine house, and prove me now herewith, saith the Lord of hosts, if I will not open you the windows of heaven, and POUR YOU OUT A BLESSING, that there shall not be room enough to receive it.

Malachi 3:10

Without tithing and giving offerings, your confessions about prosperity will have no effect. You might just as well say,

"Twinkle, twinkle little star, how I wonder what you are; up above the world so high, like a diamond in the sky"!

When God decides to honour your confessions and comes to the earth with your blessings, He will be looking for your seed. God will be looking for the seed that you have planted so that He can bless you supernaturally. But if there is no seed, what can God bless? He has nothing to work with.

It is not enough to just name it and claim it. You must go a step further and obey the Word of God. That is how you take it! You must act on your faith. Every time you give money to God, it is an act of faith. We believe that your money is not a stone, it is a seed. It is going to germinate and bring forth much fruit.

Generosity is honoured by the Lord. When God sees your acts of generosity which confirm your claim to prosperity, He will supernaturally pour out His blessings upon you.

There is that scattereth, and yet increaseth; and there is that withholdeth more than is meet, but it tendeth to poverty. The liberal soul shall be made fat: and he that watereth shall be watered also himself.

Proverbs 11:24,25

Are you confessing for a happy marriage? Then be courageous and obey the biblical instructions of marriage. If the Bible says submit to your husband, be strong and submit! You will receive many blessings because of your submission.

Husbands, decide to love your wives practically. It is not enough to confess that you have a happy marriage. It is time to take a happy marriage by obeying the Word of God courageously.

Take your miracle healing by acting on the Word of God! Believe that you have the healing and act as though you have it. If you need to take medicine in order to stay alive, then take it. But keep confessing the Word. There are times that the confessions in themselves, amount to an act of faith. God will honor your faith and prolong your life.

Are you believing God for an anointed ministry? Confess it!

In 1983, I made important confessions about my future ministry. I confessed that I was fruitful. I pronounced over my life the blessing of fruitfulness. I believe that those confessions are working out after almost fifteen years. But it is not enough to just speak. You must pray and study your Bible.

A personal knowledge of God is the greatest key for anointing. Knowing God personally is something that many ministers lack. Do you listen to tapes? If you do, you are doing something right!

But you need to go a step further and know God personally for yourself. You can have what you say, but you must act on it. Faith without works is dead faith.

What doth it profit, my brethren, though a man say he hath faith, and have not works? Can faith save him?

James 2:14

When Abraham stretched his hand to sacrifice Isaac, God saw one of the greatest acts of faith in human history. That act gave life to the promises and confessions of Abraham. Abraham had a name which meant that he would be the father of many nations. He believed that his descendants would be like the stars in the sky, the dust of the earth and the sand on the sea shore. How could such incredible things happen? Only through living faith!

Abraham's faith came alive when he courageously obeyed the Lord. Decide to obey God. Fear is what will make you disobey. If you have faith in the Lord, you will obey what He tells you to do.

In the account of the last judgement, the sheep are moved to the right and the goats to the left. It is a similar thing with your faith. The real ones are separated by the fake ones by the acts of faith that accompany them. When a confession has no confirming actions, it is actually a dead and useless claim. If you make a claim to prosperity, you must courageously go to work. You must work very hard.

The Tightrope Walker

You may have heard of the story of the man who walked across a tight rope that was tied over a waterfall. The tourists around cheered and clapped as the man performed this amazing feat. Next, the man pushed a wheelbarrow across the same tight rope. Below him was a fall of several hundred feet. This man amazingly pushed the wheelbarrow successfully to the other side. He was met with cheers and declarations of support.

He then asked the crowd, "Which of you believe that I could put a human being in the wheelbarrow and push him across this tight rope?"

The whole crowd shouted in approval saying, "We believe and know that you can do it!"

The tightrope walker then asked for one volunteer from the supportive crowd to sit in the wheelbarrow which he would push across the waterfall. There was a hush among the crowd and no one came forward. You see, the crowd claimed that they believed the man could do it, but no one was prepared to act on his claims. This meant that their faith was actually dead and useless.

If you do not back your confessions with positive actions, your faith will be a dead and useless item, worthy of the rubbish dump.

Christian friend, it is time to act on your faith. You have named it. You have claimed it. Now take it, in Jesus name!

SECTION II:

Practical Claims
and
Positive Confessions!

Introduction

In this chapter, I have simply written down some confessions that you can make. I want you to read these confessions aloud. Read them to yourself or lead others in a group confession. You will find that they inspire and generate great faith. Pastors should feel free to lead their congregations in repeating these words. I have also categorized the confessions into some familiar topics that often need the application of overcoming faith.

God called the things that were not as though they were. This chapter is full of things that may not be the case. **It is your duty to call them out as though they are already in existence.** This will cause them to come into manifestation.

> **...even God, who quickeneth the dead, and CALLETH THOSE THINGS WHICH BE NOT AS THOUGH THEY WERE.**
>
> **Romans 4:17**

Remember, you can have what you say! So speak on! Declare it! Proclaim it! You will have what you say.

> **...HE SHALL HAVE *WHATSOEVER HE SAITH*.**
>
> **Mark 11:23**

Confessions for Securing Your Breakthrough

- Greater is He that is in me, than he that is in the world!
- I have the anointing to work hard!

- The anointing for breakthrough is upon me!

- I am anointed for hard work!

- I see the anointing for new ideas break forth like never before!

- I have an anointing for excellence!

- I cannot fail because God has given me the anointing for abundance!

- The anointing for creativity is my portion!

- My ears are anointed!

- I hear the right things! I listen to the right people!

- I have the necessary information to succeed!

- My heart is anointed to receive wisdom from God!

- I am anointed!

- I have anointed eyes to see opportunities all around me!

- I have anointed hands to make my business work!

- I have an anointed mind! I am intelligent!

- The anointing of the pastor has been transferred to many faithful men including myself!

- I have a new anointing in my life!

- I have an anointing for wisdom!

Confessions for Attaining Wisdom

- I am a creative and innovative person. I have bright ideas for the present and for the future!

- My mind is alert and active!

- I am learning new things everyday in church!

- I am not confused!

- I have trusted in God and I will not be ashamed!

- The wisdom of God is better than the wisdom of man!

- The wisdom I have is the wisdom that comes from above. It is pure, peaceable, gentle and easy to be entreated!

- The wisdom I have is without hypocrisy and partiality!

- I am experiencing Solomonic wisdom!

- I have an abundance of wisdom!

- I am not a rebel. I will never be a rebel. Rebellion is not for me!

- I have wisdom for business!

- When I hear the Word of God, I immediately obey. Because of this I find myself being led by the good shepherd. When I wake up in the morning I see green pastures all around me!

- The waters nearby are still waters. There are no rough waters near me. Because I am following the wisdom of God I have no defeat or failure in my life!

- My enemies are constantly surprised at my success and breakthrough!

- My cup is running over!

- I am blessed in the morning and I am blessed in the evening!

- Wisdom has brought me promotion!

- Because I am so wise with the wisdom of God, I have been promoted!

- The wisdom of God has exalted me!

- I am moving ahead because of wisdom!

- I have wisdom for business, wisdom for school and wisdom for good relationships!

- I do not enter relationships and break up!

- I have stable and long-lasting relationships because I am wise with the wisdom of God!

- I am getting more wisdom everyday!

- I am not an old king who can no longer be advised!

- In all my getting, I am getting more wisdom!

- I seek the counsel and advice of many counsellors! Because of that I have safety in all that I do!

- I lend myself to counsel and advice!

- I will not go in the way of Judas, Adonijah, Ahitophel and Lucifer!

- I am a winner man!

- Winning ideas are flowing through my mind!

- Intelligence, insight and common sense flow through my mind and affect all of my decisions!

- Dullness, daftness and stupidity are far from me!

- The spectrum of my thoughts is wide enough to appreciate all the factors that concern me!

- The latitude of my mind and thoughts is broad enough to understand all things!

- I understand natural and spiritual things!

- I have great insight into history, geography, literature and other arts!

- I understand law, medicine, sociology and philosophy!

- I am not confused by the wrangling of false religions and deceitful philosophies!

- I know what they teach, but I do not accept it!

- My brain is not limited!

- I am a leader because I have the wisdom to lead!

- Wisdom is making me happier!

- Wisdom is making me into a better person!

- Wisdom is making me richer!

- I am not intimidated by anyone. I can relate with all kinds of people!

- From today, I have no inferiority complex!

- I can relate with managers, ministers of state and presidents!

- Many people treasure the advice that I give them. This is because I speak wisdom!

- When evil men entice me, I do not follow them into sin!

- I do not enter unwise partnerships!

- Wisdom has made me into a hard worker!

- Wisdom has made me into a man of integrity!

- I am a man of moral rectitude and uprightness!

Confessions for Mastering Your Marriage Situation

- I have found a good partner!

- I am blessed to be a married person!

- My partner is truly a blessing to me!

- I have no desires for another person!

- Contentment has filled my heart!

- I am a stable husband!

- I am a stable wife!

- On the day that I got married, several scriptures were fulfilled!

- When a man has found a wife he has found a good thing and has obtained favor from God!

- I have obtained favor with God!

- God has given me favor because I am a married person!

- Things are better for me because I am married!

- Everything I have set my hands to do is blessed because I am a married person!

- The Scripture is being fulfilled in my life everyday!

- One shall put to flight a thousand, but two shall put to flight ten thousand!

- This Scripture was also fulfilled in my life when I got married!

- Since the day I got married, my strength has increased tenfold!

- I am now driving away ten thousand demons from my life!

- Ten thousand obstacles are giving way to the blessings of God!

- I have ten times more potential for success because I am a married man!

- Marriage is not a curse to me, it is a blessing to me!

- Being married is a good thing!

- I enjoy being married!

- I am happily married!

- I maintain my confession and declare boldly that marriage is only a blessing to my life and ministry!

- My wife is a true help to my life!

- I am no longer lonely!

- My husband is dedicated to me. He has no time or eyes for other women. I am a princess and a queen to my husband. My husband does whatever I want him to do because he loves me. People envy me because my husband loves me so much!

- I pronounce that from today, God is a partner to my marriage!

- Christ is the centre of my home!

- By faith, I am not married to an unbeliever!

- My partner is a believer!

- The goodness of God is upon my family!

- I am blessed with many children. All my children are saved!

- None of my children is wayward!

- My children sing in the church choir. They are in church everyday!

- All my children's friends are good children. My children do not move around with drug addicts and smokers!

- My children are not experimenting with sex!

- None of my children is sexually active before marriage. They do not use condoms or pills before marriage!

- I will live to see my children get married!

- I will live to attend my children's weddings!

- My children will marry good and decent Christians!

- They will marry in an honorable way and will not disgrace the family!

- The grace of God covers my children!

- No evil comes to my house!

- My child is outstanding in school!

- My child obtains good results in school!

- I have overcome the curse of divorce in my family!

- No spirit of separation can enter my household!

- I have an ideal family!

- There is peace in my home!

- I have overcome the spirit of continuous quarreling!

- Quarrels have died down in my house!

- I am experiencing peace and happiness!

- My partner is faithful to me!

- I am not afraid of unfaithfulness!

- I know that he is faithful to me!

- I will not commit adultery. I will not become a piece of bread!

- By the grace of God, I will make it to the very end!

- I have completely broken up with all past relationships!

Confessions for Eradicating Marital Problems

- My home is like a garden of peace and tranquility!

- My husband comes home at the right time every day!

- My husband is not a drunkard!

- There is no alcohol in my home!

- Our family finances are getting better everyday!

- Our family is becoming richer everyday!

- There is enough money to pay the rent, electricity bills and water bills!

- We are not in debt!

- Everyone in this family reads his Bible and prays everyday!

- Although my husband may be an unbeliever, I confess boldly that he is saved from today!

- My husband has no power to sleep with other women. I satisfy him everyday!

- I declare that my husband is only interested in me and no one else!

- I pronounce that I will not get any disease through my husband's unfaithfulness!

- I close the door to gonorrhea, HIV and other venereal diseases!

- My husband spends his money on me and not on girlfriends!

- I have no financial lack!

- I halt every unfaithful practice of my husband with any outsider!

- I declare that any lady who steals my husband will receive the judgment of a thief!

- I see their destruction. I declare destruction, disgrace, terror, panic and confusion on every woman that is trying to take my husband from me!

- I will never divorce. I will remain married to the very end!

- Every spell, enchantment or bewitchment that has been conjured against me and my marriage will not succeed!

- I will not separate from my husband!

- My partner and I live in the same house. We sleep in the same room. I declare that we lie on the same bed everyday!

- We are happy together. There is sweet love in our house everyday!

- Anyone who stands outside our window will hear the sound of crackling laughter and joy everyday!

- There are no beatings, quarrels, shoutings or slappings in my house!

- There are no slaps and insults in my house anymore!

- I cannot slap my husband. My husband cannot slap me!

- I cannot slap my wife. My wife cannot slap me!

- There is a lot of mutual respect and love in the house!

- My husband and I do not have sexual intercourse with our servants, colleagues or friends. We are faithful to each other!

- We commit love with each other on a regular basis!

- All men that see me know that I am called by the Lord God and that He has blessed me!

Confessions for Entering Marriage

- I have no fears in me. I shall be married in this life!

- I declare boldly that marriage is for me!

- I will not be a bachelor or a spinster for the rest of my days!

- God has given me a good partner!

- Good men are proposing marriage to me right now. It is happening practically in my life right now. I declare it to be so right now!

- My days of waiting are over!

- I am free from panic, terror and family harassment because I am not married!

- I maintain that every spiritual condition has been made for me to have a good partner!

- Every curse in my life that is preventing me from getting married is broken from this very moment!

- I declare that I am free from spiritual curses and bondages that prevent people from getting married!

- I will not struggle to find a partner. I will have a choice. I am not a hustler. The days of struggling are over. Here comes my husband! Here comes my wife! I see him/her practically now! He/she is in my life today!

- God has provided someone just for me!

- I can see a ring on my finger!

- My wedding day has arrived!

- I confess boldly that I am the bride!

- I see my wedding day. I see the flowers. I hear the wedding bells. I see the crowds. My Saturday has come at last!

- My days of loneliness are over. My days of walking alone are over. I come to church with my husband/ wife. My children are following me. I see them practically in my life today!

- I am delivered from making a wrong choice. I will not marry the wrong person. I will marry the right person!

- I will not be deceived. I have the wisdom for making right choices. The Spirit of God is leading me to take the right decisions!

- From today I will seek the kingdom of God. As I seek the kingdom of God, all other things, including husbands/wives shall be added unto me. I see them being added now!

- God is adding good things to my life!

- I am building God's house. As I build God's house, God is building a home for me. A home of peace. A home without loneliness. A home without tears. A home without sorrow. A home of joy. A home of laughter with my spouse!

- I see myself cracking jokes with my spouse. Things are so nice and I am so happy. I see it now! It is real! And it is happening practically today!

- I am not marrying for selfish reasons. I am marrying for biblical reasons!

- I am keeping myself pure. I will not live in fornication before marriage!

- I do not have unbeliever boyfriends or girlfriends!

- I have the Spirit of faith and patience. Because of this, I have supernatural ability to believe and to wait!

- El' Shaddai is changing the course of my future. He is providing what was impossible!

- My enemies are surprised at how God has provided for me!

- Those who thought I would never marry are bewildered at how God has blessed me!

- My enemies are baffled, dazed, astonished, confounded, stupefied and flabbergasted!

- My reproach has been taken away and they cannot believe it!

- I insist that I am as blessed as Abraham!

- I cannot fail. I cannot be defeated or disgraced. It is happening for me now!

- I am entering into my Promised Land, in the name of Jesus!

Confessions for Breaking and Family Curses Bondage

- I have a new family in Christ. I belong to a heavenly family!

- I declare boldly that ancestral and familiar curses have no hold over my life!

- I believe that Christ has set me free and I am free indeed!

- I am free from the oppression of the devil through my family!

- I have freedom from family vices like drunkenness, immorality and infidelity!

- I am free from the spirit of poverty that is in my family!

- I have victory over the spirit of polygamy, quarrelsomeness and backwardness!

- The curse of family diseases has been broken in my life!

- I am no longer subject to hypertension, sickle cell disease, asthma or heart attacks!

- Every mental disease and depression in my family has no effect on me whatsoever!

- I distance myself from witchcraft power and occult spells and enchantments that are over the young people in my family!

- Although one thousand people in my family may be under the curse of infirmity and poverty, Christ has set me free from that road!

- I break myself free from every family habit and attitude. I have the right attitude!

- I am not irksome, quarrelsome or cantankerous!

- I have a sweet spirit and a gentle disposition. I am a nice person to be with!

- Tribal curses, as far back as ten generations, have no power over my life today!

- National curses of poverty and continental curses of poverty and backwardness have no effect on me!

- I cannot be suppressed!

- God has made me the head in my family!

- My brothers and sisters have seen that God has called me!

- My future is bright. I have become a creator of wealth!

- I am not an eunuch. I have descendants after me!

- I am plenteous with goods and my goods shall pass on to the generations that come after me!

- My household is planted by the rivers of water!

- I belong to a winning family; the family of God!

- I am far from the wickedness and oppression of Satan!

- My household and I shall serve the Lord. We shall live long and we shall prosper. We shall have no lack!

- I belong to a progressive family!

- I am only going forward!

- I reject outright discouragement, disgrace and despair. These things are no longer a part of my family!

- The blood of Jesus joins me to a better family. Because of the blood, I have a new name and a new family!

- I am free from the curse of chronic diseases in my family!

- I have overcome the curse of hatred in my family!

- I am free from the curse of my ancestors!

- I am free from the curse of idolatry in this nation!

- I am not under the curse of starting and never finishing!

- Financial bondages are broken in my life!

- Every family and generational curse is broken from as far back as ten generations!

- I am not afraid of anyone in my hometown!

- There is no spell, enchantment or power that has power over me! Who is it that saith a thing, and it cometh to pass when the Lord commandeth it not!

- Anyone in my village who casts a spell against my life will be extinguished and overruled immediately!

- A witch cannot fly over my house anymore. If any witch attempts to fly, it will never fly again. I say, it will never fly again!

- Witchcraft powers in my hometown are afraid of me. They know that I am covered in the blood. They know that I have protection. Because of the blood, destruction will pass over and will never harm me!

Confessions for Overcoming Wicked and Unreasonable People

- I believe and confess that I have good friends in my life!

- My friends are more than my enemies. My enemies have no power over my life!

- In spite of what people say against me I am prospering and succeeding!

- I proclaim that my enemies are disappointed and disgraced!

- I have overcome unreasonable and wicked men!

- People who have made themselves into impossible and unmovable elements will suddenly be removed.

I predict their sudden transfer. I pronounce that every
unreasonable and impossible human being in my life
is being divinely displaced from his secure position. I
see them being replaced!

- Wicked tormentors all around are being displaced
  and replaced on a daily basis!

- Confusion has entered into the camp of my enemy!

- I declare that my enemies shall reap what they sow!

- They that sow lies against me shall reap confusion,
  hatred and death!

- The neck of my enemy is broken. The tongue of my
  tormentor is crushed!

- I have the mastery and the victory over unyielding
  men and women who use their authority against me!

- I am divinely protected from the hatred of powerful
  people!

- I cannot lose my job suddenly. I shall not lose my
  position!

- God has established me. What God has given to me,
  no one on earth can take from me!

- Those that betray me shall be executed!

- All things are working together for my good!

- God is exposing my enemies. I see my enemies
  fighting against each other. They will come against
  me in one way, but they will scatter in seven different
  ways!

- God is revenging all evil that has been done against
  me!

- For every bad story that has been spread against me,
  God is giving me ten more good testimonies!

- God is giving me a good name to supernaturally replace the poison that has been spoken against me!

- Every setback I have experienced will work out for my promotion!

- The sword of the Lord is in my hand!

- Like David, I shall destroy every Goliath in my life. I see every Goliath falling down before me. It is difficult to fight against me because God is on my side!

- Greater is He that is in me, than he that is in the world. Because He is in me I cannot fail. I have overcome them because He is in me!

- Anybody who rejects me will regret it later. Those that despise me will bow down before me. Some of my enemies will live to see my day of promotion and exaltation. Some of my enemies will not see my promotion, for they shall be cut off in the midst of their years!

Confessions for Experiencing Prosperity

- I believe in fantastic prosperity!

- From now, God will have pleasure in my prosperity. I believe and confess that God is happy when I prosper. Because of this, I am prospering all the time. I am prospering everyday!

- I have discovered that prosperity is not an evil thing!

- I embrace the concept of prosperity wholeheartedly!

- I recognize that God wants me to flourish. Because of this, I am stable, planted and expecting to prosper!

- I decree prosperity and increase in all the work of my hands!

- I am a house owner. I am a builder of houses!

- I see myself acquiring land and building a house. It is a good thing to build a house. God's Word tells me to build houses and to plant gardens. Therefore, I am building houses and planting gardens!

- God has given me the wisdom to build a house free of debts and curses!

- My house is a beautiful mansion. The finishing of my house is exquisitely appealing. People admire my house everyday!

- All the rooms in my house are filled with good and precious gifts according to the book of Proverbs!

- I have garages in my house. In my house, the garages are filled with the latest and best types of cars in the world!

- I am a car owner. Prosperity is coming into my life. The days of walking are over. I see myself driving a good car!

- God has promoted me and the impossible has become possible!

- I believe and confess that I have a car, and that I have more than one car. I even give away cars as gifts!

- God has prospered me so much that a car means nothing to me anymore!

- I believe in hard work. I have the spirit of diligence. I am not a lazy person, I work very hard. And I reap what I sow!

- I am free from the curse of working for nothing. I break the curse of laboring in vain. My sweat is not in vain. I reject every thought of poverty and lack.

I refuse every projection and prediction of poverty by my family!

- I will not become what people think I should be. I will become what God says I am!

- God has made me the head and not the tail!

- I am plenteous in goods!

- I am plenteous in increase and in profits!

- Supernatural doors are opening. When God opens the door, no human being can shut it!

- I am not struggling to prosper. I am enjoying God's prosperity!

- My prosperity is real. I owe no man anything!

- I make genuine profit and I am debt free!

- I own buildings. I have real estates!

- I have moved into fantastic prosperity!

- I confess that God supplies all my needs according to His riches in glory!

- I have nice clothes to wear!

- I eat good food everyday!

- I have a good job. My job is getting better everyday!

- The impossibility is becoming possible!

- Prosperity does not make me backslide!

- In spite of the fact that I am blessed, I go to church regularly. I attend prayer meetings and fasting sessions!

- I am not stingy. I give freely. Even when I do not have I give willingly!

- I am always scattering, yet I am always increasing.

Men are giving back to me good measure pressed down, shaken together and running over!

- I am reaping a hundredfold. I am enjoying abundance. It is happening practically in my life!

- My future is clear and bright. I have bright eyes for the future!

- The windows of heaven are open over my life!

- I command supernatural abundance over my life!

- I declare that I am flourishing like a palm tree!

- I am content with what the Lord has done for me. I have a Spirit of contentment. I do not have greed in my life!

- I am like a tree that is planted by the rivers of water. I am bringing forth fruit in the right season!

- I declare that I have the right contacts, supplies and opportunities. They are mine from today!

- Whatever I start, I will finish. All my projects are completed. I am a finisher!

Confessions for Obtaining a Mega Church

- My church is growing. My church is growing in beauty and in excellence!

- My church is prosperous!

- We have no lack of members and souls. We are experiencing a continuous harvest of souls!

- We claim the anointing for soul winning, miracles and church growth for ourselves!

- Our churches everywhere are growing!

- There is growth everywhere. There is blessing everywhere!

- There is joy in this church. There is peace. There is harmony. There is unity!

- I see a fresh anointing coming. It is coming. It is coming like a cloud into the church!

- The enemies of the church are disappointed. They are disgraced. They have lost their jobs. All of those who expect our downfall will be disappointed!

- We see and declare a divine displacement and replacement of evil men in high places who fight against the church!

- We declare the judgment of God on people that fight against God!

- The enemies of the cross have come to nought!

- Signs and wonders are happening in the church. Notable miracles are occurring everyday!

- It is a great thing to be a part of the church. Many more people are coming to the church. They come from the North, South, East and West!

- Members of our church are not disgracing the Lord!

- I am a pillar in the church. I am a pillar in this ministry. I am a great support to this vision!

- I have a spirit of loyalty. I am consistent, faithful, dependable and constant!

- My pastor depends on me and I never disappoint him!

- My church is so large that thousands upon thousands of people belong to it. God has given us a Mega Church. We have become a nation within a nation!

- The church is respected and honored in the community. The love of God is breaking through!

- The power of prayer and the power of confession are working wonders in the life of the church!

- Rebels, tergiversators, anarchists, mutineers and breakaways cannot destroy what God is doing on a daily basis!

- Rebels will only experience continuous disgrace. I will not join a rebellious movement within the church!

- I love my pastor because he tells me the truth!

- I will not be angry with the pastor anymore!

- When I think that the pastor is preaching about me, I will resist the lie of the devil to be angry with my leaders!

- My pastors have a great vision and I will not leave this great ministry!

- They that are with us are more than they that are against us!

- Amazing miracles of healing regularly take place. Wheelchairs are emptied in our church!

- The blind see in our church. The deaf hear in our church. The cripples walk in our church. Cancer victims are healed in our church. The miraculous is a daily occurrence in our Mega Church!

- We have a Mega Church. God has promoted us. We have been lifted out of a classroom. We have our own church building!

- More and more people are coming to the church!

- Anybody who associates with our church is blessed. Anyone who comes to our church will come again.

When they are returning, they will bring more people!

- I declare that people are rushing to church every Sunday. There is no space for people to sit anymore!

- I have a problem of space to contain the crowds that God has given me!

Confessions for Accomplishing Great Things in Ministry

- I declare boldly that I am called of God to be a minister of the Gospel!

- I was not called by a man; I was called by God Almighty!

- I am faithful to my calling. I will remain steady, committed and consistent to the specific calling on my life!

- I will not deviate into politics, church rivalry or rebellion!

- I will respect my teachers and seniors who have trained me in the ministry!

- I declare boldly that I have not finished learning. I have a servant attitude. Because of this, I experience blessings everyday!

- My ministry is developing because I am still developing. I read important books and listen to tapes regularly!

- I demonstrate my commitment against ignorance by reading the books of other ministers. My ministry is greatly enhanced because I am constantly learning!

- I am not an old king who can no longer be advised!

- I experience success in ministry!

- I am a man of integrity, uprightness and moral and financial rectitude!

- I am not a thief of God's money!

- I do not live a wasteful and extravagant life!

- I am not a disgrace to the call of God!

- I am not in the ministry for filthy financial gain!

- I am not a fornicator or adulterer. I do not have sexual affairs with my church members. I am walking in holiness everyday!

- My wife is ordained to stand by me. She helps me in the ministry. Every spirit of quarrels and opposition is removed from my wife, in the name of Jesus!

- My wife does not scatter my church members anymore. She helps to gather!

- I have good assistants who are loyal!

- All separatists, dissenters and breakaways cannot succeed in destroying my ministry. Like Judas, they shall fall into their own traps!

- I have a culture of loyalty in my ministry!

- Righteousness prevails in all that I do!

- I shall not divorce my wife or husband. The ministry will not destroy my marriage!

- My children will grow up to serve the Lord. They shall do great exploits for the kingdom of God. My children will not be drug addicts or cocaine dealers. They will serve Jesus from an early age. All my daughters will be virgins when they marry!

- My ministry shall continue in beauty and excellence!

Confessions for Achieving Pastoral Success

- I am a pastor of a glorious church. Behold the glory. I see glory everywhere!

- I declare that my church experiences prosperity all the time. There is no lack or need in my ministry!

- All my deficiencies are covered by the blood!

- God supernaturally helps me to overcome my limitations. My limitation in education cannot keep me from going forward in the ministry!

- My church does not borrow money!

- My church members give generously to the ministry. Most of my members pay their tithes!

- I am not an extortionist. I do not manipulate my church members to get their riches!

- I do not put on a show of poverty. I am self-sufficient. I am well paid. I do not behave like a beggar who is in need of a tin of milk or sardines!

- I do not need people to feel sorry for me anymore, God has blessed me!

- My ministry is reaching the unreached. I am a soul winner!

- When I get to Heaven, I will receive a soul winner's crown. Because I am in the ministry, many people will be saved. Many people will go to Heaven because of my ministry!

- I have good worship leaders in my church. I have a beautiful choir. God has given me loyal musicians!

- Every aspect of the church is working well because God has blessed me with good people!

- I am a successful pastor!

- I treat my associates well!

- I pray for my assistant pastors. My pastors are more and more anointed than they have ever been. They have peace and long life. Their enemies are truly scattered!

- I declare that those in the forefront of this ministry have divine protection. The Lord will fight for them. The Lord will keep them from political intimidation and attacks!

- Of all that the Father has given me, I have lost none. On the day of Judgement, I will be confident!

- I can feel the anointing increasing. I am moving into higher realms of ministry. I receive invitations to minister from around the world!

- God gives me divine protection. I am blessed going and I am blessed coming. I am blessed in the city and I am blessed in the field!

- By faith, every attack on my ministry shall be quenched. I shall prevail!

Confession for Dominating in the Business World

- From today, God is my business partner!

- I am a lender of money and not a borrower!

- From now, God uses me to help the work of God financially. I declare that I contribute millions to the work of God. I confess boldly that one of my goals is to support the work of God!

- Jesus is the lover of my soul, and I am a lover of Jesus. I declare that I love Jesus more than I love money!

- Jesus is the Lord and Master of my business. God will reward me this week with success and breakthrough. God will reward me this week with victories and answers!

- Everyone that owes me money will pay me from today!

- All of my investments are safe and secure!

- Every broken wall of business and marriage, I command to be restored right now!

- I see a new abundance in my life!

- Divine ideas, divine insight is flowing through my mind!

- I have financial miracles everyday!

- I am so rich that I don't know what to do with my money!

- As I sow my first and best fruits and tithes, I declare that the windows of heaven are opening in my life!

- My barns are filled with plenty!

- My bank account is full. My bank account is bursting. This is because I pay my tithes regularly!

- I am not greedy!

- My pockets are overflowing with money!

- The bank manager respects me because I have a prosperous bank account!

- God is using me to help the poor and the needy!

- I have won important contracts. I continue to win major contracts!

- I am not a liar. I am not a thief. I do not engage in crooked deals. I do not engage in bribery and corruption!

- In spite of the difficult economic climate, I experience abundance!

- I give with simplicity!

- I am not trying to control the church because I donate large amounts of money. I am not trying to be noticed because I donate large amounts of money. I donate large amounts of money to the church because I want to be a blessing to God's kingdom!

- I do not go for loans to impress people with flashy cars and mobile phones. I need to impress no one!

- My business is not built on debts!

- Because God is with me, I see when evil is coming and I keep myself safe from the power of economic recession and depression!

- I am a substantial person!

- I am not a man of straw. I am a man of true wealth. I am a man of riches. I am a man of gold and silver!

- I am not ashamed of the blessing that God has given me!

- I am free from arbitrary confiscation and intimidation by jealous government officials. I am free from harassment by covetous dictators who wish to bring me down!

- I am not afraid to prosper!

- I pay my taxes regularly. I fulfill all my obligations. And I am blessed everyday. I am building houses everyday. I believe in building houses. Because I build, I experience permanent and real prosperity!

Confessions for Overpowering Demons and Witchcraft

- Christ has set me free and I am free indeed!

- I have authority over witches and wizards. I am not afraid of occult powers!

- I am delivered from the demon of inferiority!

- I am free!

- I am free from the demons of self-pity!

- I am delivered from the control of demons of jealousy and envy!

- I take authority over the spirit of depression!

- I am no longer depressed. I can see the way forward!

- The power of witchcraft is broken!

- I have hope for tomorrow!

- I bind the demons of discouragement in my life. From this moment, every demon of discouragement leaves me!

- From now, I pronounce and declare my freedom from anxiety!

- I am no longer harassed by the demons of worry!

- The spirit of fear and restlessness is bound!

- I declare that the demon of fear no longer leads me!

- I am loosed and I am free because Christ has set me free!

- I am free indeed!

- I have power over demons of unforgiveness and bitterness!

- I have overcome the spirit of bitterness and hatred in my life!

- I love all men!

- From today, I love my enemies!

- I am free from the power and hold of deception!

- I pull down every stronghold of satanic intimidation in my life!

- I am loose from evil curses and bewitchments on my family!

- Christ has conquered Satan and has defeated him on the cross. Because of this, I walk in freedom from the powers of darkness!

- The shackles of Satan are dropping off me!

- There is no charm from my hometown that can affect me. Every spell and enchantment against me emanating from my village is overruled!

- I release ministering spirits and angelic powers to contend with my spiritual enemies!

- Demonic spirits in the form of human beings have no power over my life!

- I am free because Christ has set me free!

- I am blessed and not cursed!

- The doors are shut and demons can no longer enter into my home!

- I undo the curse of perpetual problems. I have overcome problems that do not want to go away!

- I reject the spell that keeps my car constantly in the workshop!

- I drown the enemies of my life in the red sea!

I command my enemies to be disunited and fragmented!

- I paralyze the invented plans and decisions that are taken against me everyday. I refuse to enter a coffin before my time. I cancel the dreams that put me in a coffin in the name of Jesus!

- I reject the spell that keeps my property in the possession of someone else. I enjoy all my inheritance from today in the name of Jesus!

- Every prolonged sickness has been healed now!

- I pronounce that I am free from the power of alluring strange women!

- I have overcome the power of unending problems!

- I overrule and overthrow the power of persistent and perpetual calamities, miscarriages and unexpected death in my family!

- I cover myself with the blood of Jesus!

- I refuse to die in a car or plane crash!

- I am free to live beyond the curse of demonic limitation of life!

- I have authority over mental disease, epilepsy, schizophrenia, and depression. None of these plagues have any power over my life anymore!

- The door is shut by the blood of Jesus. And the charms cannot affect me!

- I abort the wicked plans of the enemy for my life!

- I terminate every satanic agenda and prediction that is against my life!

- I cause a divine abortion of every plot and invention that is set against me!

- I confound every form of invented logic that is contrary to my life and ministry!

Confessions for Operating Successfully in Life

- I am blessed with Abraham's blessings. I am blessed in the morning. I am blessed in the evening. Abraham's blessings are mine!

- Impossible situations have been turned around in my favour!

- My promotion is here!

- God has shown me His favour!

- I believe that God has given me constant favour in all the work of my hands!

- I have outstanding results in my school!

- All things are working together for my good!

- God's promotion is real to me!

- I cannot be defeated anymore!

- Silver has become to me like stones!

- I am experiencing Solomonic Success!

- I am experiencing Abrahamic Success!

- I am experiencing Davidic Success!

- Excellence in business and excellence in school is my portion!

- I am blessed with clothes!

- I am blessed with food and raiment!

- I am no longer a failure. I am above and not beneath!

- I am a blessing to my family and to my church!

- Anyone who blesses me is blessed!

- Anyone who curses me is cursed!

- I enjoy "the corn, the oil and the wine" of this earth!

- My latter end shall be greater than my beginning!

- Although my beginning is small, my latter end shall be greatly increased!

Confessions for Subduing the Opposition

- The Lord is with me as a mighty and terrible one!

- The Lord is with me and He will never leave me!

- My persecutors are about to stumble. I see my persecutors falling before my face!

- They shall kneel down before me and pay homage to me!

- My oppressors shall be greatly ashamed. They are about to be disgraced!

- According to the Word of God, my tormentors shall have no peace in their beds. They shall not prosper. I see them experiencing confusion!

- The vengeance of the Lord will hit them suddenly. They will cry out in pain and scream for mercy!

- The Lord is a mighty one and He is on my side!

- Every enemy that rises against me this week, shall fall for my sake, in the name of Jesus Christ!

- I reverse every evil word spoken against my life from today!

- I refuse bad news and evil tidings because I am blessed and highly favoured!

- The walls of opposition that the enemy has built have come down!

- Every mountain of opposition has become a mountain of blessing!

- Every lie fabricated against me will come to nought. It will be proved that the stories against me are lies. Those things will turn out for my promotion!

- My enemies speak evil of me. They sit together and discuss me. They ask themselves: "When shall he die and his name perish?" All that hate me whisper together against me. Against me do they devise my hurt. They say, "An evil disease cleaveth fast on to him." They say, "Now that he lieth he shall rise up no more." Mine own familiar friend in whom I trusted has lifted up his heel against me. But the Lord shall be merciful to me!

- I have been raised up by the Lord. God has favoured my cause!

- My enemy cannot triumph over me. God has set me before His face forever more. God has delivered me!

- All those that seek after my soul are being driven backwards right now! They are being put to shame at this very moment!

- The Lord is thinking about me right now and has put a new song in my mouth!

- I see myself coming out of a horrible pit. My feet are being taken out of the miry clay. God is setting me on a rock right now!

- God is establishing me in life, business and marriage. Many shall see it and fear and put their trust in theLord!

- God has not forgotten me!

- I will not continue mourning because of the oppression of my enemy. I rise up now and praise my God!

Confessions for Crushing Spiritual and Physical Enemies

- God has delivered me from wicked and unreasonable men and women!

- Bad things are happening to my enemies. God is fighting against those who are fighting against me!

- I see the Angel of God standing up to help me. The Angel of the Lord has drawn out his spear to contend against the enemy!

- My enemies have become like the chaff of the wind. They are turning away into confusion!

- The Angel of the Lord is chasing my enemies!

- I am delivered from unreasonable people!

- I boldly declare that the way of my enemies is dark and slippery!

- Those that have fought against me without cause and those who have dug a pit for me without cause shall be destroyed!

- I see destruction coming upon my enemies. Every net that my enemy laid for me shall be used to catch himself. Into that very destruction he shall fall. I see him falling now!

- Every false witness against my life who said evil things   about me, shall be rewarded for his evil!

- Any person who has rewarded my good favors with evil, shall experience perpetual unhappiness!

- Those that rejoice against me and gather themselves together against me shall gnash their teeth. They are being destroyed by the Lion of the tribe of Judah!

- From today, my enemies cannot wrongfully rejoice over me!

- Every disloyal person who is devising evil against me shall be brought to dishonor. I see my enemies being swallowed up in shame!

- God has filled my mouth with shouts of joy. God has filled my heart with rejoicing!

- All my enemies are being clothed with shame and dishonour because God is pleased to destroy them!

- My salvation is not in numbers!

- The chariots are prepared for battle but safety is from the Lord!

- The name of the Lord is my refuge and I shall not fear!

Confessions for Overcoming Disappointment and Emotional Problems

- The Lord is my light and my salvation!

- Rejoice not against me, O my enemy!

- When I fall I shall arise!

- Although it seems that I am down today, the Lord is raising me up right now! I will not be down forever!

- This disappointment will turn around for my good!

- This setback is working out for my advancement!

- The Lord is my light. Although it is dark around me, I see the Lord lifting me up!

- I am not afraid of the darkness!

- The heaviness in my heart is gone!

- I will shed no more tears. My days of crying are over!

- I shall not be sad forever!

- I boldly declare that this experience shall work together for my good!

- My life is moving ahead!

- I will not be depressed anymore. In fact, I am not depressed anymore!

- No man can break my heart. No human being can break my heart!

- My trust is in the Lord who is my strength and my salvation!

- I am pressing on!

- This experience is a stepping stone!

- This complex situation is a stepping stone to my blessing!

- All things are working together in my favor and for my good!

- My enemies are being used to promote me!

- The Lord is the strength of my life. I don't feel weak anymore!

- Disappointment has no power over my life!

- Depression has no power over my life!

- Grief has no power over my life!

- Every trace of sorrow, fear, terror and panic is gone from my life!

- No man on this earth can frustrate my life!

- I am not a frustrated person!

- I am a blessed person!

- I am flourishing!

- Things are getting better with every passing minute!

- I feel myself rising!

- I declare that I am rising above every experience in my life!

- Everyday is a learning experience for me. I have learnt my lesson!

- I will not make those mistakes anymore!

- Improvement has come into my life!

- Although everything around me seems bleak and hopeless, my heart shall no more be afraid!

- I am confident!

- From now on, I will desire one thing. I will desire the Lord!

- I will seek after the Lord. Early in the morning, I will come to the Lord. I will seek for Him in the evening!

- From now on, I will dwell in the house of the Lord all the days of my life!

- I see God setting me upon a rock!

- I see God hiding me in His tabernacle!

- From this moment, I am safe. I am secure!

- I see God lifting up my head. God has lifted my head high up above my enemies who are round about me!

- I can see the light at the end of the tunnel!

- After every night, there must be a day. My day is coming!

- I see the sun rising on my life!

- I know that it looks impossible but I'm rising again!

- I am beginning to sing. I'm singing praises to the Lord!

- I'm rejoicing in the Lord!

- I would have fainted. I would have died. But because I believed I see the goodness of the Lord!

- God is showing me His goodness right now!

- Things are getting better!

- I have hope for my life. I have hope for the future!

- I shall not be ashamed because the Greater One is in me!

Confessions for Overcoming Complex Situations

- There are complex problems all around me, but my God is bigger than all of them!

- Although there are troubles around, God is bringing me out of all my distresses!

- There is no mountain too big that God cannot move it. I see this mountain of bitterness and betrayal moving away from me right now!

- I see this difficult situation melting away!

- I see that mountain of impossibility in my life vanishing!

- God has rescued me from complicated and unusual difficulties!

- Although I have been betrayed, God will never disappoint me. Because God will not disappoint me, I have hope for the future!

- God never fails, and God will never fail me!

- I see God exalting me now!

- The end of my life is only peace and joy in the Holy Ghost!

- I see wicked people who seem to have great power. The wicked man seems to spread himself like a big tree. But I predict today that he shall pass away. He shall disappear like the chaff of the wind!

- I see the Judas in my life withering and fading away!

- I have overcome every setback!

- I bring down every unscriptural and wicked expectation of my enemies for my life!

- I disappoint and reverse every satanic claim and demand on my life!

- My future is bright!

- I superimpose the purpose of God and the brightness of God on my circumstances!

- I superimpose goodness and mercies over betrayal and wickedness!

- I cannot stay down forever!

- I bring down every wall of resistance in my life!

- I declare boldly that the complex nature of my problem will not keep me down. I have risen above it from this moment!

- I am free. I am free!

- I overrule the decisions that have been taken against my life and business!

- I nullify every death wish and wicked expectation of hypocrites in my life!

- From this moment, I am not afraid of tomorrow. I can face tomorrow!

- I am not afraid of the unknown. I have control of the unknown, in the name of Jesus!

- There is no invisible power that can frighten me any longer!

- All decisions that have been taken against me by my enemies are nullified and cancelled in the name of Jesus!

- Every meeting that is held to plan my destruction is frustrated in the name of Jesus!

- I stop the accusing finger that is pointing against me!

- I cannot be down forever. Joy cometh in the morning!

- Rejoice not against me O my enemies!

- I am rising. I am rising now. I am going forward!

- I silence the voices of unkind and diabolical slanderers. They have no power over my future!

- I am covered in the blood of Jesus!

- My future is bright!

- Every stumbling stone has become a stepping stone!

- What made me stumble is what is making me progress!

- I replace every frustration, failure, defeat, disorientation and disorganization with victory, breakthrough, stability and success!

Confessions for Bearing Much Fruit

- I am fruitful in every aspect of my life!

- I am fruitful spiritually!

- I am fruitful physically. I have no problem with childbearing or fertility!

- God has made me fruitful!

- I am abiding in Christ. I am staying in the church. Because I am staying in the church and in Christ, I am always bearing much fruit!

- I am doing well spiritually!

- I bring many people to Christ everyday!

- When I get to Heaven, Jesus will say to me, "Well done, good and faithful servant"!

- I have overcome the distractions that prevent people from bearing fruit!

- I am not distracted into other unnecessary things!

- I read my Bible everyday. I pray everyday. I have my "quiet time" everyday. And I bear much fruit everyday!

- Through me, my colleagues in my office have been born again!

- Through my life, my colleagues in school have come to know the Lord!

- Through my life, people I meet in buses and taxis are born again!

- When I stand at the bus stop I bear fruit!

- When I am in my office, I bear fruit!

- When I am in school, I bear fruit!

- I am always leading people to Christ!

- I invite people to church on a regular basis!

- I am not a hypocrite. My life as a Christian does not drive people away from God!

- I bring people to Christ because they see in me Christ-like behaviour!

- I do not have any spiritual disease. I am spiritually healthy!

- I am a real Christian!

- Christ is working through me!

- I abide in Him and He abides in me!

- Whatever I ask of the Lord, He does for me!

- The Lord has made me plenteous in goods, plenteous in the fruit of my body and plenteous in the fruit of my hands!

- I am blessed in the city and blessed in the country!

- The Lord has given me His good treasure!

- My business is a good business!

- The heavens over me are open. I see the rain coming down over the land!

- I am like a tree planted by the rivers of water!

- At the right season everything works out perfectly for me!

- I have children. I have spiritual children. I have physical children. The Lord has blessed my bank account. My bank account is full everyday!

- I am blessed in the fruit of my body. My children are blessed. They are good children!

- My handbag and wallet are blessed!

Confessions for Improving Yourself in Prayer

- I declare boldly that my spiritual life is taking a new turn!

- Prayer is no longer lacking in my life!

- I pray on a regular basis!

- I pray for at least one-hour everyday!

- I speak in tongues on a regular basis!

- When I am walking or driving I speak in tongues!

- Whenever I pray in tongues, I am edified!

- No one understands me, however, in the Spirit I speak mysteries to God!

- Because I pray in tongues regularly, I am becoming a mighty spiritual warrior!

- My spiritual life is improving at this very moment!

- Because I pray regularly, I do not yield to temptation!

- There is a great improvement in my prayer life!

- I no longer find it difficult to wake up early enough to pray!

- I pray the prayer of agreement and I experience results!

- I pray for the nation and its leaders. Because of this I live a godly, peaceful, and honest life!

- I regularly pray for the kingdom of God to come!

- My mind and heart is always on the church of God and its leaders!

- I pray for my pastor that God will establish him and have mercy on him!

- I ask the Lord for whatever I need and He answers me!

- I lack nothing in my life because I have one hundred percent answers to my prayer!

- Whenever I pray I forgive those who have wronged me. Because I always forgive them, God is forgiving me everyday!

- There is no bitterness in my heart when I pray!

- I am definitely improving in my spiritual prayer life!

- God delivers me from temptation everyday!

- God delivers me from evil all the time!

- A thousand are falling on my left and ten thousand on my right hand side, but nothing bad happens to me. This is because I pray that God should deliver me from evil and lead me not into temptation!

- I can now pray for several hours. I can pray for one continuous hour. I can pray for two continuous hours. I can pray for three continuous hours. I can pray for four continuous hours. I can pray for five continuous hours. I can pray for six continuous hours. I can pray for seven continuous hours!

- God is taking me to higher heights in spiritual things!

- I fast on a regular basis because Jesus fasted!

- Jesus Christ predicted that we would fast. Because of this I fast regularly!

- Just like Apostle Paul, I fast often!

- Whenever I fast, I make time to pray!

- Prayer and fasting gives me great results!

- I have breakthroughs in my life everyday!

Confessions for Mastering the Word of God

- The Word of God is sweet. It is sweeter than honey to my mouth. That is why I read my Bible everyday!

- I have a Bible. I read my Bible all the time!

- I do what my Bible says I should do. I always obey the Word of God!

- I can do what my Bible says I can do!

- I have what my Bible says I have!

- I am what my Bible says I am!

- I am more than a conqueror. I am blessed. I am healed. I am delivered. I am rescued. I am saved. I am victorious. I am above. I am not below. I am the head. I am redeemed. I am sanctified. I am the righteousness of God. I am what the Bible says I am!

- I do Bible study on a regular basis!

- I do microscopic and topical Bible study on a regular basis!

- I am not a shallow Christian because I study the Word regularly!

- I am not an empty Christian because I meditate on the Word of God everyday!

- When I meditate on the Word of God I become wiser!

- I have invested in Bibles!

- I have different versions of the Bible!

- Oh, how I love the Bible!

- It is my meditation all the day!

- Through meditating on the Bible, God has made me wiser than my enemies!

- I have more understanding than all my teachers. For thy testimonies are my meditation!

- Thy Word is a lamp unto my feet, and a light unto my path!

- The entrance of God's Word gives light to every aspect of my life. I know what to do because the Word gives me direction!

- My steps are ordered because of the Word of God. I am a good man/woman and my steps are ordered by the Lord!

- In the Word, God has shown me what is good and what He expects me to do!

- I constantly listen to tapes!

- Because faith comes by hearing and hearing by the Word of God, my faith is improved when I listen to tapes!

- I see myself becoming a spiritual giant right now!

- I have great faith because I am always soaking in the Word of God!

- Because I love the Word of God, I experience great peace. Nothing offends me anymore!

- My eyes stay awake in the night that I might meditate on the Word of God!

- I read Christian books on a regular basis and they are helping me greatly!

- I fight against ignorance in my life by reading books. I am not an ignoramus. I am wise, intelligent and learned!

- By the power of meditation, I rise into success!

- The Word of God does not depart from my mind. I meditate on it everyday. Because of that, I experience success in my life!

- I have divine insight and divine revelation in the Word of God!

- The purpose and calling of God on my life will b fulfilled!

- I am growing as an individual!

- I am growing in the Word of God. I am growing in the Holy Spirit. I am growing in my character!

- My life in public is the same as my life in secret!

- I destroy every secret sin, evil and wickedness in my life!

- I remove every skeleton from my wardrobe!

- I am clean outside and I am clean inside!

- The glory of God is fresh on me!

- This present glory is upon my life!

- I am faithful to the church!

- The church is marching on and the gates of hell cannot prevail against us!

- The enemies without and the enemies within cannot stop us!

- I see something new!

- I see continuous beauty, continuous excellence and continuous prosperity!

- This church is a source of direction and inspiration to many lives!

Confessions for Cancelling Debts by Faith

- I declare that by the grace of God I am debt free!

- I owe no man and I am blessed because I owe no man!

- My business and life do not depend on loans and debts!

- Christ has set me free from the curse of debts!

- According to Deuteronomy 28, it is a blessing to lend and not to borrow. From today, that is my portion!

- I am a giver and a lender. I am not a borrower!

- I am free to walk in town. I am not terrified by warning letters, phone calls and angry creditors!

- I owe no man!

- I am so blessed that when people come to pay me I give it back to them!

- All outstanding bills and unpaid debts are cancelled in the name of Jesus. This is my faith and I declare it boldly. It shall come to pass practically in my life!

- I am not broke!

- I am not down!

- I am not under!

- I am above!

- My business is succeeding!

- My life is improving!

- The things in my house are not acquired by debts!

- I really own the things I have!

- I do not owe any of my fellow church members anything!

- I am free from the curse of debt!

- I don't owe any money!

- From today, I am free from the yoke of debt!

- Christ has set me free from the bondage of financial traps!

- Every trial of the devil upon my life has turned into a testimony. I have many testimonies. Testimonies of healing and victory!

- Every mountain in my life is flattened in the name of Jesus. I declare that every crooked path shall be made straight. The mountain of impossibility has become possible in the name of Jesus!

- I have overcome the curse of poverty from perpetual debts in the name of Jesus Christ. And I am redeemed from all of my problems!

Confessions for Developing Loyalty and Faithfulness

- I live a pure life in holiness and righteousness!

- Members of our church have lifestyles of holiness!

- My friends are good people. I am a good person in public and in private!

- Stability is a main characteristic of my life. I am stable!

- I am loyal. I am faithful. I am dependable. I am reliable!

- I am here. And I am here to stay!

- I have breakthroughs in my life because I am stable!

- The spirit of criticism and gossiping are no longer in my life!

- Satan is the accuser. Because of that I shall no longer accuse and judge anyone!

- I do not want to be like Satan!

- I have broken the Judas' spirit in my life!

- I am delivered from rebellion and disobedience!

- I am not resistant to the voice of God!

- I am not part of any insurrection in the church!

- I kill every attitude of defiance in my life!

- I reverse every stubborn spirit in my life and ministry!

- I am not part of any mutiny, sedition or insurgence in the church!

- I am not a rebel. I am not a separatist. I am not a breakaway member!

- I shall never be part of a revolt or guerilla movement within the church!

- I am a loyal, faithful and dependable servant!

- I do not have a double tongue. What I say is what I mean!

- I am not a man pleaser!

- I am not position conscious!

- I will not be a Judas by the grace of God!

- I have the anointing for loyalty, unity, stability and consistence!

- Because I am faithful, God is promoting me everyday!

- God is lifting me up everyday!

- I do not withhold information from my pastors and leaders!

- When I hear of insubordination and slander I will report it to my spiritual leaders just as the family of Chloe reported divisions to Apostle Paul!

- Loyalty will cost me some relationships and friendships. But I am prepared to pay the price!

- Because I have the attitude of a humble and loyal servant, God is giving me a double portion of the anointing!

- I see the anointing coming on me!

- I feel the anointing dripping on me!

- I see God's blessings of promotion and upliftment coming on me right now!

- Because I am faithful with that which is another man's, God has given me my own blessing!

- Because I am faithful and loyal in that which is little, God has given me that which is much!

- I am faithful with money. Because I am faithful with unrighteous mammon, God is giving me the true riches of His anointing!

Confessions for Overcoming Persistent and Habitual Sins

- I am free from worry, self-pity, condemnation and stress!

- I do not worry about unnecessary things anymore. I have cast all of my burdens unto Jesus. I am now burden free!

- I am free. I am free from delusions, hallucinations and evil spirits. I no longer hear voices speaking to me and accusing me!

- The spirit of hallucinations has no power over my life. I silence the voice of the devourer that is harassing me!

- I dissolve the yoke of hallucinations and delusions and mental imaginations that are contrary to the Word of God!

- My mind is clean and pure. Evil thoughts have no place in my mind anymore!

- I am no longer frightened by dreams, imaginations and suggestions of the devil!

- I am covered in the blood of Jesus!

- Although I have sinned in the past, the blood of Jesus covers me. I am forgiven!

- I no longer sleep in church when the preaching is going on!

- I insist on my freedom from the bondage of overeating. I can fast from today!

- I announce that I am free from the power of scorning, backbiting and criticizing in the name of Jesus!

- I am free from the persistent problem of gossip, criticizing and scorning!

- I am not proud. I have overcome the problem of making boastful remarks!

- I am a free person and I am happy because God is good to me everyday!

- I have overcome the spirit of tiredness when it comes to the work of God. I do everything in the name of Jesus, whose I am and whom I serve!

- I no longer have a problem of fornication!

- I am not a womanizer!

- I will not sleep with any man or woman anymore. I am not an animal. I respect myself. And I will do what is decent and right!

- I am not a homosexual!

- I do not practice any form of homosexuality. I do not accept it. I will never accept it because the Word of God rejects it as an abnormality!

- I will no longer commit abortions!

- I am not a murderer. God has forgiven me for shedding blood!

- My mouth is free from lying!

- I am free from the sin of stealing. I no longer have to take that which belongs to someone else!

- I am not covetous!

- I have overcome every spirit of backsliding in my life. There are no symptoms of backsliding in my life!

- I will not fall, I will stand. I will stand because Jesus will help me to stand!

- I am experiencing regular fellowship. I am not an irregular Christian. I am dependable!

- I am delivered from old habits that hinder me from serving God!

Confessions for Developing a Righteous Lifestyle

- Jesus died for me on the cross. His blood has cleansed me from all unrighteousness!

- I am determined to walk in holiness!

- I am holy by the grace of God!

- God is searching my heart and trying my thoughts!

- I am constantly praying that God will remove every wicked way from my heart!

- I am keeping my heart with all diligence!

- I do not allow evil thoughts to enter my mind!

- I am His workmanship. I am a new creation!

- I do not sin anymore!

- I have been created for good works. I practise these good works on a regular basis!

- God has separated me from a wicked and perverse generation!

- The grace of God that brings salvation has appeared to me. Because of this, I am denying ungodliness and worldly lusts!

- I declare boldly that I will live soberly and godly in this present world!

- I have constant victory from today over the power of addiction to tobacco, cigarettes and alcohol!

- From this moment, hatred, bitterness, murder, anger, insults, swearing and foul words are taken away from my life. I permanently separate myself from these vices, in the name of Jesus!

- I do not have an uncontrollable temper!

- My mind is free from filthiness and contamination!

- The fruit of the Spirit is operating in my life from this moment!

- I can say "No!" to the devil when I am tempted!

- From this moment, I will say "No!" to the devil when he tempts me!

- I am not a strange woman. I will not cause the fall of any Christian brother or man!

- I will not curse myself by sleeping with somebody's husband!

- I will not lead anybody into sin!

- God is revealing his plan to me!

- I am constantly aware that the Holy Spirit is in me!

- I am now experiencing the fruits of the Spirit in my life. I am developing the character of holiness, joy and peace in the Holy Ghost!

- I live in righteousness and purity all the days of my life!

- I am not a bad person. I am a good person!

- I am a kind and upright person in the name of Jesus!

- I am patient with unreasonable people. I am a nice person!

- I do not burst out in anger and irritation all the time! I have a nice character!

- I am constantly yielded to the character of the Holy Spirit!

- I am blameless and the husband of one wife. I am the wife of one husband!

- I am not self-willed or given to wine!

- I am not a lover of filthy money that comes from corruption!

- I am not ill-natured or cantankerous anymore. Even if that is the nature of my natural family, I separate myself from that character, in the name of Jesus!

- I am not a quarrelsome or troublesome person. I am not unruly and I am not a liar!

- I am a solid, dependable and faithful Christian. My pastors can depend on me!

- Whether they see me or not, I will be doing the right thing!

- I am known in the church. I am a sheep that is near to the shepherd. I am not a sheep that is far away!

Confessions for Victory

- I project and predict victory in all that I do and say!

- I am happy because God is on my side!

- I cannot fail because the Greater one is in me!

- Jesus told me that He will be with me. Because He is with me, I cannot be vanquished!

- If God is for me, who can be against me!

- If God is for me, with me and in me, what evil can succeed against me!

- In all these things, I am more than a conqueror!

- I am convinced that neither death nor life nor angels nor principalities nor powers can separate me from the winning touch of God!

- I am persuaded that neither entities nor powers, nor things present, nor things to come, nor any other creature can prevent me from experiencing my blessings in Christ!

- I declare that every battle I am facing has turned to my favour. Things are working out in my favour!

- Every enemy that rises against me this week, shall fall for my sake, in the name of Jesus Christ!

- I reverse every evil word spoken against my life from today!

- I refuse bad news and evil tidings. Therefore I am blessed and highly favored!

- God has freed me from disgrace!

- I don't have unbeliever boyfriends or girlfriends!

- I have freed myself of all bad company!

- I command the multitude of problems before me to disperse, scatter and disintegrate in the name of Jesus!

- I cannot be defeated anymore!

- I am not confused!

- I am not unhappy!

- I am no longer discouraged. I am not depressed. From now, I am encouraged and stress free!

- I speak to every dark area in my life and command the light of God to show the way!

- No danger comes near my dwelling place!

- I refuse to worry from today!

- I reject unbelief and anxiety!

- I pass all of my exams. I overcome all temptations, trials and tests. In the time of famine, the Spirit of God gives me wisdom!

- I pass all my exams!

- School is not a problem for me anymore. I do well in every subject!

- I predict excellent results in every future exam. I am the head and not the tail. I am the first and not the last!

- I overcome all temptations, trials and tests. In the time of famine and difficulty, the Spirit of God gives me wisdom!

- I am a winner. I have winning ideas. I have winning solutions!

- God is causing me to have victory all the time!

- I am the head and not the tail!

- My life has a purpose!

- Impossibilities are becoming possibilities!

- For me to fail, God has to fail. Because God cannot fail, I will not fail!

- The spirit of laziness is gone!

- All around me is peace. He is helping me, He is there!

- No evil tidings come near me. Those that wait to hear bad news about me will wait forever. There shall be no bad news about my life!

- God has set His love on me. He will deliver me. He will set me on high!

- When I call on Him, He answers me. He is with me in trouble!

- He will honor me with long life!

- He will satisfy me and show me His salvation!

- Angelic powers and heavenly forces are loosed for my sake everyday!

- I am defended on every side by the powers of Heaven!

- I am safe by the blood!

- Because of the Spirit, the water and the blood I predict absolute victory in every situation!

Confessions for Capturing Happiness and Peace

- I know the Lord and the Lord knows me!

- Because I have found Christ, my life is peaceful and happy!

- I have no more worries!

- My lips shall greatly rejoice in the Lord!

- I will sing praises unto my King. Because I have found the Lord, I have need of nothing else!

- God has done great things for me. God is doing great things for me!

- Although men take counsel against me and say, "God has forsaken him", I know that God has not forsaken me!

- Jesus has promised that He will not forsake me!

- The conclusion of my life is simple - to serve God and to keep His commandments. From today, my life is to serve God and to keep His commandments!

- Peace is mine. Joy is mine. Everlasting happiness is mine!

- I am surrounded by the excellent beauty of God!

- God has given me riches and wealth!

- God has given me the power to eat thereof and to take my portion!

- God has given me the ability to rejoice in my labour and to be happy in my life!

- God has blessed me so much that my soul wants nothing!

- My soul is filled with God!

- I shall die in a good old age. And I shall go to my grave in honour!

- I have applied my heart to know wisdom!

- The end of my life is better than the beginning!

- Better things are in store for me. I have great hopes for the future!

- I shall lie down and experience the rest of God!

- When I sleep I have only good and sweet dreams!

- I do not experience frightening dreams that cause me to panic. I do not see cows, snakes or antelopes chasing me!

- I absolutely reject every dream of myself in a coffin. I am not in a coffin. I am alive. I am well. And I am blessed!

- Although many people are envious of me, I continue to prosper!

- I succeed in spite of the hatred of my enemies!

- I will not die suddenly!

- The doors that have been shut in my life, are beginning to open. Doors of marriage, doors of happiness, doors of peace, and doors of riches!

- I will live to a good old age!

- I see into the future!

- I am becoming a leader in the house of God!

- I am respected in the church. I am respected in the Christian community!

- I see the way forward now!

- I have peace all around me. I am no longer frightened by the giants around me. I am not a grasshopper!

- I see solutions. I see solutions. I see breakthroughs. I see breakthroughs!

- I see happiness. I see joy. I see peace. I see blessings. I see promotion. I see a lifting. I see answers. I see

contentment. I see tranquility all around. I am truly
in green pastures. I am truly by the still waters!

Confessions for Your Healing

- Surely He has borne my griefs, my sicknesses and my
weakness. He has carried my sorrow. Christ Jesus has
taken away my pain!

- We considered Him smitten and afflicted by God, but
He was wounded for our transgressions. He was
bruised for our iniquities. The chastisement of our
peace was on Him and by His stripes we are healed!

- I see myself healed by the stripes of Jesus. The price
has been paid. I shall not carry this disease any
longer!

- I am not afraid. The Lord will strengthen me and
protect me. He will heal me from every strange
disease!

- The Word of God is pleasant to me. It is sweet to my
soul and health to all my bones!

- I shall attend to the Word of God. I shall not let them
depart from my eyes. I shall keep the Word of God in
the midst of my heart!

- For the Word of God is life to me and health to all my
flesh!

- Abraham prayed for Abimelech, his wife and his
maidservants and they bore children. The God of
Abraham is alive today! I shall also bear children!

- According to Exodus 15:26, none of the diseases of
the Egyptians have any power over me. He is the
Lord that healeth me!

- I am serving the Lord my God and He shall bless
my bread and my water!

- Sickness has been taken away from my family! Sickness has been taken from my home. I don't see sickness any more, I don't see tragedy any more!

- I will not have a miscarriage. I will not be barren. I am fertile. I have as many children as I want!

- I will not die before my time, I will fulfil my days. I shall not die in this hospital. I shall be discharged in the name of Jesus!

- My days are prolonged. My life has been extended. The blood of Jesus protects me from evil diseases!

- Many are the afflictions of the righteous, but the Lord delivers him out of them all. I see the Lord delivering me out of my afflictions right now!

- No evil shall befall me. No plague or calamity can happen to me. I declare it to be so, in the name of Jesus!

- I bless the Lord for all His benefits, He has healed me!

- He sent His Word and healed me. I have been rescued from the grave in the name of Jesus!

- My broken heart is healed because He is a healer of broken hearts!

- I see myself renewing my strength. I see myself rising up right now. I see the darkness clearing away. Joy cometh in the morning. I see joy coming right now!

- Like the woman with the issue of blood, I am healed today. Years of sorrow are no more. I shall no longer spend money on doctors!

- I shall no longer suffer in hospitals. I am healthy. I am whole!

- I have touched the hem of His garment and I have been made whole!

- Every evil spirit of cancer, every incurable disease is broken in Jesus' name!

- The Kingdom of God is at hand. Kingdom blessings are happening to me every day!

- Heal the sick, cleanse the lepers, raise the dead, cast out devils, freely ye have received, freely give. These commands are happening practically in my life today!

- I see a miracle ministry. I see healings taking place all around me!

- The blind see, the lame walk, the lepers are cleansed and the deaf hear!

- The dead are raised up in my ministry and the poor have the Gospel preached to them!

- I am not afraid of death. I believe that God will heal me and raise me up. I will believe in God until the very end!

- These signs are following me every day; healing the sick and casting out demons!

- Demons are no problem to me. All that are vexed with unclean spirits are healed. I have overcome the spirit of mental illness!

- God is doing special miracles in my life. Handkerchiefs and aprons are taken from my body and they drive out evil spirits!

- There is an anointing to break curses right now!

- I am free from fever, inflammation and burning sensations!

- God has healed me from acute leukaemia and strange blood diseases!

- I am healed of iron deficiency anaemia and megaloblastic anaemia!

- African trypanosomiasis and schistosomiasis have no access to my life!

- In the name of Jesus Christ, I terminate every life threatening disease in my body! Acute severe asthma, sickle cell crisis and Grand mal epileptic attacks have ceased!

- I am free from madness, blindness and astonishment of heart!

- I dissolve every form of stone formation in my kidneys, bile ducts or salivary glands. Kidney stones, gall stones and salivary stones are being dissolved right now!

- I absolutely reject every form of cancer within my body. I totally refuse entry to any malignant cells. I completely abort any form of strange growth within my body!

- I command the following cancers to die immediately: prostate cancer, cancer of the uterus, cancer of the cervix, cancer of the lungs, cancer of the bone and cancer of the brain. I shall not die from cancer!

- I cancel every form of cancerous growth in my life. I terminate all and every kind of malignant cancer in my life. I speak death unto breast cancer, stomach cancer, liver cancer, kidney cancer, intestinal cancer and cancer of the pancreas!

- Every form of epilepsy, be it Temporal lobe epilepsy, Grand mal epilepsy, Petit mal epilepsy or Jacksonian epilepsy is cured instantly in the name of Jesus!

- I predict and pronounce freedom from every psychiatric condition. I am completely cured of schizophrenia, severe depression and mania!

- I declare that every suicidal tendency in my life is permanently cured. Hallucinations, delusions and illusions are things of the past. Psychotic illnesses and neurotic symptoms have disappeared from my life. My mind is clear, I am healed and I am normal!

- I am free from anti-anxiety drugs, mood stabilizing drugs, anti-depressant drugs, and anti-psychotic medication!

- I am delivered from acute confusional states, memory disturbances, difficulty in thinking, psychomotor changes and emotional disturbances!

- Alzheimer's disease and every other form of dementia is completely abolished in my life!

- I boldly declare that I am healed of alcoholism and the power of cannabis sativa (marijuana). Every toxic confusional state of drug abuse is permanently cured in my life!

- Cocaine, amphetamines, morphine and heroin and every hallucinogenic drug has no attraction to me from this hour!

- I am not afraid of anything. I am free from every kind of phobia, anorexia nervosa, and every stress related disease!

- I have a perfectly healthy personality. I overrule, override and cancel every anti-social personality, paranoid personality, dependent personality, histrionic or hysterical personality, schizoid personality and obsessional personality in my life. I have the personality of Christ!

- I am not overweight. I am not underweight. I eat normally. I do not have a problem of over-eating!

- Every pain in my body is healed instantly; neck pain, shoulder pain, elbow pain, hand and wrist pain , hip pain, back pain, waist pain, knee pain, foot and ankle pain are healed at this moment. It happens right now in the name of Jesus!

- I terminate every form of malaria parasite in my body. I sentence the following malaria parasites to instantaneous death: Plasmodium falciparum, Plasmodium vivax, Plasmodium ovale and Plasmodium malariae!

- Every form of chloroquine-resistant malaria is abolished right now. I declare that typhoid fever is cured right now. No form of fever can attack me in the name of Jesus!

- I am cured by the power of the stripes of Jesus. Every form of arthritis disappears from my body at this moment. I command rheumatoid arthritis, ankylosing spondylitis, psoriatic arthritis, and chronic osteo-arthritis to disappear in the name of Jesus!

- I pronounce my healing from strange and incurable diseases. Systemic Lupus Erythematosus, Progressive Systemic Sclerosis, Multiple Sclerosis, Poly-arteritis nodosa are cursed from my life in the name of Jesus!

- I am free from heart diseases. My heart beats normally. Chest pain, heart attacks, myocardial infaction, angina pectoris are all healed in the name of Jesus!

- I am cured of atrial fibrillation, cardiac arrest and heart block in the name of Jesus Christ!

- My lungs are perfect. I am cured of tuberculosis, pneumonia and asthma!

- I am cured of every kind of worm. No worm can survive within my body from this moment. I terminate the life of tape worms and round worms in the name of Jesus!

- The following worms have been sentenced to death within my body: Taenia saginata, Taenia solium, Enterobius vermicularis, Ascaris lumbricoides, Trichuris trichiura, Necator americanus,

- Ancylostoma duodenale, Strongyloides stercoralis, Capillaria philippinensis, Wucherena bancrofti, Brugia malayi, Loa loa, Onchocerca volvulus, Dracunculus medinensis (guinea worm), Toxocara canis, Ancylostoma brasiliensis, Oesophagostomum specis, Angiostrongylus cantonensis, Trichinella spiralis, Gnathostoma spinigerum, Anisakis marina!

- I have a normal pregnancy and the baby within is growing normally. It is not suffering from retardation of growth or any other abnormality!

- I predict and declare that I shall have an easy and swift labour. My baby shall be delivered with great ease. I cancel every malposition and malpresentation of the baby!

- I shall not suffer from face presentation, brow presentation or breech presentation of the baby!

- I shall not die during labour. I shall live to look after my child. I shall not bleed to death after delivery!

- I am free from Pregnancy-induced hypertension, Renal disease, Eclampsia, Anaemia, excessive blood loss, abnormal labour or abortion!

- I shall give birth to an intelligent and healthy child. My child is healed of congenital heart disease and rare inherited illnesses!

- I refuse to suffer from diabetes mellitus, thyrotoxicosis, hypertension, heart disease, asthma or mental disease!

- I thank God that I enjoy the full benefits of divine health and long life!

- I enjoy miracles of healing everyday!

Confessions for Travelling

- I am blessed going and blessed coming!

- The chariots are prepared for battle, but safety is of the Lord!

- The angel of the Lord encamps around me as I travel today!

- I cannot die in a car accident in the name of Jesus. I am safe from drunken and reckless drivers!

- No evil shall befall me as I go out today!

- I am not a victim of careless driving and reckless disregard for human life!

- I am being guarded by angelic powers. I am safe on the land, on sea and in the air!

- I have arrived safely at my destination. I shall return home safely to my family!

- I abort and terminate every plot and device of Satan to kill me or hurt me on this journey!

- I bind every occultic power, enchantment or spell on any part of the road!

- There is no enchantment against Jacob and there is no devination against Israel!

- A 1000 cars and planes may crash at my left hand, and 10,000 at my right hand, but I declare that I shall not be on-board any of them!

- My plane or my car shall not be hijacked!

- I am safe from armed robbers, hijackers, serial killers, lunatics and rebels!

- This is a very prosperous journey. I am receiving favour at every corner. My pockets are full of blessings!

- My spiritual life is improved by this journey! Because of me, everyone is safe on this journey!

- Thou I walk through the valley of the shadow of death, I am not afraid!

- My car is roadworthy. The police shall not arrest me on the way!

- I cover myself and all my loved ones with the blood of Jesus Christ. The blood of Jesus shall answer every demand and claim for my life today!

Confessions for Sound Sleep

- The Lord gives His beloved sleep!

- From today, I enjoy my sleep. I no longer struggle to sleep at night!

- I am not afraid of the night anymore!

- I have sweet dreams from today. I cancel every bad dream from this moment. I no longer suffer from strange nightmares!

- I arrest every witch who dares fly over my home. My home is a no-fly zone for witches and wizards!

- No arrow that flies by night can affect me anymore!

- I don't need sleeping tablets anymore. I am free from all tranquilizers and sedatives!

- I no longer see coffins and graves in my sleep. I override every negative and terrifying dream in the name of Jesus!

- Cows, monkeys, snakes, crocodiles and every strange creature will no longer chase me in my sleep!

- Evil spirits do not and cannot harass me at night!

- I terminate every spiritual and sexual encounter in my sleep. I no longer have sex with strange people or beings in my dreams!

- I do not oversleep anymore. Laziness is no more a problem for me. I am able to wake up when I have to!

- I no longer wet my bed!

- I no longer have wet dreams!

- From today, I cover myself and my household with the blood of Jesus!

- I am safe from rapists, thieves and armed robbers!

- No bad person visits me anymore. Every thief within my household shall be exposed!

- The angel of the Lord encamps around me. I am safe in his hands. I enjoy peaceful and blessed sleep!